Fuel Stop

Finding Power, Energy & Support for Life's Journey

Joan Fleming

Jorjeanna Press
Minneapolis, Minnesota

FUEL STOP © copyright 2004 by Joan Fleming. All rights reserved. No part of this book may be reproduced in any form whatsoever, by photography or xerography or by any other means, by broadcast or transmission, by translation into any kind of language, nor by recording electronically or otherwise, without permission in writing from the author, except by a reviewer, who may quote brief passages in critical articles or reviews.

ISBN 0-9644484-1-6

Library of Congress Catalog Number: 2004108228

Cover and interior design and typesetting: Mori Studio

Cover photo: The Roses in a red convertible. From the left: Mary, Joan, Jacque and Sue

Printed in the United States of America

First Printing: July 2004

08 07 06 05 04   6 5 4 3 2 1

To order, send $16.95 plus $2.00 shipping and handling to:
Joan Fleming
8705 Rambil Road
Eau Claire, WI 54703

quantity discounts available for 10 or more copies

For Anne, Kate, Meg and Molly

When I am with you the sun shines!

Contents

Preface *vii*

1 A Journey with Friends *1*

2 Recharge Your Batteries *29*

3 Every Car Should Have a Compass *59*

4 Spark Plugs *83*

5 Some Traveling Companions *101*

6 Help, Don't Honk! *113*

Acknowledgements *119*

From My Bookcase *122*

Preface

When is the last time you sat around, in your pajamas, with a group of women and laughed so hard you wet your pants?

How long has it been since a woman friend wrapped her arms around you and told you it would be all right and you would survive whatever your latest crisis was, and you believed her?

Have you ever looked into the eyes of a dear friend who was dying, knowing this would be the last time you would ever see her? Your words to each other had been spoken. You knew that you'd soon experience a feeling of emptiness that would last your lifetime.

Have you ever thought about why some of your relationships with women confidantes, often beginning when you were girls together, are some of the most precious in your life?

How often have you pondered the mysterious and magical bonds between mothers and daughters?

As wonderful as these relationships can be, they too can be fraught with pain, half-truths and facades as we humans attempt to protect fragile egos and present a face to others that we believe they will somehow approve of. Who among us does not want to be well thought of, included and liked?

And yet, when the facades are put aside and we are willing to disclose our fears as well as our joys, we often see a mirror reflection of ourselves in the eyes of the women we trust. Who among us does not want to be more fully understood?

During such intimate conversations, we begin to feel more empowered, increasingly energetic and warmly supported. What if, I began to wonder, I could expand the circle of women's experiences even further? What if I could put it all in a book?

Those are the questions that led to this book. My purpose in writing this book is to offer life experiences and words that might make your life experience a little sweeter.

I named this book *Fuel Stop* because three definitions of fuel are power, energy and support. These characteristics have the capacity to expand what's in all of us—our inner strength.

They are not my words or stories alone, but those of many other women. You'll discover, as you read, the wisdom of ordinary women and personal choices they made in their lives. Some are uplifting and others are painful. You might feel a kinship with some of the women and question the sanity of others.

I've included some poetry because women can often speak most eloquently when writing. Throughout, you'll read about simple pleasures women have dreamed up for family as well as friends and there will be, at the end of each chapter, ways to increase deeper communication between women who are trying to reach out to each other. And if you sometimes laugh out loud, I won't tell anyone you wet your pants. As you'll find out in Chapter I, "It's under the rose."

For the past thirty-five years I have presented workshops for women from Alaska to Hawaii. In the beginning these workshops had to do with self-esteem, family communication and goal setting. These workshops were largely the research of other people. Along the way I discovered my passion and a woman who attended a workshop led me to it.

I had asked the women, "How are you different when you are feeling especially good about yourselves?" I heard many fine responses, from "My insides match my outsides," to "I feel more abundant and enjoy the success of others, rather than envy them." The one that reached furthest into my insides was, "I am much more creative and imaginative about myself and my life!"

Well! And don't many of us strive for that feeling?

That one comment led to my workshops entitled *Zestful Women!* I talked to hundreds of women and have drawers full of notes so that I wouldn't forget their words. I asked them what they did for themselves, adventures they had with family members and friends that gave them the fun of planning, the joy of doing, and later, the glow of beautiful memories. I have included several of their experiences within these pages.

Here's what they taught me. Zestful women are:

- Women who will take the time to reflect about what is truly important to them and, acting on their chosen values, take the action to make things happen.
- Women who have the courage to become emotional risk takers, in expressive words as well as the growth that comes from venturing out of comfort zones and security blankets.
- Women who never lose touch with their playful, young, girlish natures and are willing, on occasion, to allow them freedom again.
- Women who fully understand that their women friends can keep them from the bridge when the pain is great enough to want to take a leap.
- Women who build and preserve traditions, understanding the legacy they will leave for future generations.
- Women who are growing in spirituality and believe that their life has meaning beyond what is possible to comprehend during this lifetime.
- Women who relish life.

You'll meet plenty of zestful women in these pages. I'm pleased to have you along. Enjoy the trip!

Chapter One
A Journey with Friends

> "The most beautiful discovery true friends make is that they can grow separately without growing apart."
>
> *Elizabeth Foley*

I relish the idea of women's slumber parties. When I was young and in high school, the thought of spending a night away from home with my girlfriends was delicious. Now, at sixty-nine, when memories of my friends come into my conscious thoughts, I often feel such tenderness about our shared vulnerability at that age that I want to wrap my arms around them and tell them again how much they meant and still mean to me.

I have been a part of several women's groups during my life and, although the choices we have made may vary greatly, what we have in common is monumental. We search for ourselves amid the expectations of others and often define ourselves beginning with the experiences of our mothers. We all want to be understood by a few people who will empathically listen and we want our relationships to be vital and loving. As we age, it becomes increasingly important to build a legacy that will reflect our values and our spirits so that future generations may come to know and remember us.

Looking back, I see now that being a part of a group of women has been a constant in my life. Each group, coming at different stages of my life, has brought different gifts. You may find that some of my friends bear a strong resemblance to yours.

High School and the Big Four

My high school group was known as the Big Four. We were all tall and lanky—around 5'7"—and, as our name implies, there were four of us: Dorothy, Pat, Joan and Joan.

We spent our high school years in a small Wisconsin town of about one thousand people. I moved there with my family when I was in the eighth grade and being the new girl in town, I was both excited and frightened.

I remember my father driving our family to this small town for the first time and sensing what a big change was about to occur in my life. I also remember pouting and some tears as I slunk in the back seat of our car, taking quick looks out the side window. It's hard enough to be a thirteen-year-old girl and it's tough to be the new girl in a sea of strange faces. My insecurities told me that others would be critically examining me and I was pretty darn sure I wasn't going to measure up. Within weeks, however, three girls welcomed me and the Big Four was born. By the end of that first summer we all had matching red cotton jackets and thought we were hot spit, but we were hot spit only on the outside, as we were about to discover together, when our talk took us below the surface of our facades.

What brings girls together? Why do we often know within hours or days who our comrades will be? I don't know the answers. It could be magic or chemistry or fate. I do know how grateful I was to be accepted by them and how good it felt to be with them. I discovered a sense of belonging and the beginnings of who I was and who I would become.

Competition between us consisted of comparing our legs to see who had the best set to trying out for the same parts in high school plays, since that was an interest we shared. When Dorothy got the prize role of Antigone, while I was relegated to Ismene, Antigone's sister of fewer lines, I was crushed. I was despondent for a few days before realizing that just being in a play together was great fun.

Those were the days and years of either ecstasy or despair and all of us could switch from one end of the spectrum to the other in minutes. On so many occasions, we were each other's safety nets.

I believe, although the passage of time may have distorted some memories, that we had few snits between us. Girls of that age need each other. Looking at our close friends we often see reflections of ourselves and the support we can give each other is monumental. I remember concerned faces when I suffered humiliations and disappointments. I remember how keenly they listened when I needed so badly to be understood. I believe I did the same for them. I know I wanted to. Their presence told me I didn't have to muddle through my teenage years alone.

We had other friends, of course, but the combination of the four of us somehow allowed for trust well beyond any other relationships. We would sit around a campfire pledging that we would be best friends forever.

Dorothy would often talk about her yearning for adventure. If nothing else, and since money was an issue, she would tour the world on a banana boat. She was a bottomless pit for adventure and her laugh was infectious. I can still see her, in my mind's eye, skating on the frozen river behind my house. In her early teens, she was attempting difficult movements, over and over, until she was satisfied.

Pat's nurturing capabilities were evident at an early age and there were many children and adults who benefited from her compassion.

We all shared an interest in Speech and Forensics and for Joan this meant reaching out of a comfort zone. She always had a very private side and listened rather than talked a good share of the time. It was usually up to the other three of us to pry her loose from her toothbrush and get on with the day's adventure. She brushed longer than anyone I've ever known. Her humor rose to the surface when she dramatically mimicked a woman getting dressed—bra, garter belt and girdle-twisting and turning in ways only another girl or woman could understand. She broke us up every time she performed.

All of us shared a great interest in theatre and a general dislike of girls' physical education classes. Girls in the late 1940s were not encouraged to be athletic. A couple of us had our periods more than once a month to escape the torture of communal showers and our ugly gym outfits.

One of our most passionate discussions was about our mothers. Were we like or unlike them? ("Tell me the truth.") Were they happy? Their lives seemed so mundane in our small town. We all grew up in very modest homes and had somewhat different role models in our mothers. Dorothy's mother was a teacher and my mother worked side by side with my father in a Gambles store while Pat and Joan's mothers were homemakers.

We talked about our four mothers' involvement in our town's most prestigious women's group—the Two Hour Club. This group met once a month for two hours and following lunch, the members took turns presenting an educational and informative half hour. The only other women's groups were church related and, painfully, the women had to be voted in to the Two Hour Club. Our mothers all made the cut. When we compared notes we discovered that each of them fretted about what they would wear on club afternoons. They'd be in an absolute tizzy when their turn came to arrange the program of the month although their biggest challenge came when the group met at their home. Horrors! What would the other women think about the way their homes were decorated—or, in my mother's case, not decorated. Were they serving a dessert that compared favorably to last month's offering? The pages of their *Joy of Cooking* cookbooks were dog-eared and well used.

We all instinctively knew our mothers never felt quite good enough and always took a back seat to the wealthier women. I still remember my mother talking about Ev's white Hanmaker suit.

From our young perspectives, we couldn't identify at all with their anxieties. Who cared about living room furniture, tea sets and fancy desserts?

This is what I believe to be true in hindsight: what did seep into the unconscious brains of the Big Four and dig a deep hole, was to always strive to meet the expectations of others and to never feel quite good enough. We didn't understand how their homes were a reflection of them. Like Margaret in the TV program, *Father Knows Best*, their lives were judged by the food they prepared, the homes they invited other women into and the outward success of their husbands and children.

In my home, our dining room buffet was usually covered with schoolbooks, an assortment of clothing and anything else no one in the family had time to put away. On the days when the women of the

Two Hour Club came, our buffet was polished to a sheen and held two candles and a bowl of waxed fruit.

You know what we girls didn't talk about? We never mentioned or dreamed about any possible careers we might want to pursue. Instead we talked about what our children's names might be, what kind of a house we might live in, and what our future husbands might be like.

I don't know what visions for themselves may have lain dormant in the souls of my three friends—dreams and hopes that were not connected to relationships, but to personal growth. I think we never talked about such things because we couldn't put words to these unfamiliar feelings or perhaps we were embarrassed to express them, even to each other. Most probably they were crowded out because of the importance of what was happening in the moment. I believe girls of that time, seeking approval from others, often pushed their own needs and desires to a deep place in their souls and many years may have passed before these dreams fought their way to the surface or died.

We paged through a book entitled *The Naked and the Dead*, searching for the juicy parts. We were, of course, more interested in the naked. That was the extent of our sex education. That and the word, NO.

We believed we were expected to lead lives very similar to our mothers and follow the governing societal rules of Midwest America. We would become, in the proper order: married with children, wives and mothers, cheerful and complacent women.

We had a teacher, Malina Verich, who was an anomaly in our small high school. She taught Latin, was the Forensics coach, directed all the school plays and taught the girls' physical education classes. Her mission was enlarging our world. Her small Latin classroom held photos and posters of theatre in New York, ballet in London and opera in Milan along with art throughout the world. What dolts we were! We simply could not relate to the world at large. Our world of football games, who would ask whom to the prom and who recently broke up with whom filled our heads. And yet I still think of Miss Verich today. I would like her to know that not all of her seeds fell on barren soil. Some seeds just took a little longer to germinate.

Our high school years flew by and when we started college, all going to different places, we soon found we were growing apart. I remember, one Christmas vacation, my father telling me that we would all find new friends and that was the way life was. I had expressed my sadness to him, saying it just wasn't the same between the four of us anymore. Still, the relationships we had formed lingered.

I was the first to be married, leaving college after just three semesters. Dorothy told me, years later, that following my wedding the three of them talked about their sense of loss. The Big Four was no more.

The years following marriage, children and moving around the country kept the four of us apart until we were in our mid-forties. Then came a holiday season when Dorothy and I re-connected. Over the years we had kept in touch with each other but our paths never allowed for more than the occasional card or phone call. During the short, but joyous, time Dorothy and I had together we planned a reunion of the Big Four that would be held at my cottage on a lake in Northern Wisconsin the following June.

Pat was all for it, but I regret to say the other Joan declined.

Dorothy and Pat visited Joan only to find she had little interest in our upcoming reunion. We knew her life had taken a tragic turn at the death of her husband and she was in a place that demanded solitude and healing. We felt a sadness that our group was missing a woman we would have loved spending time with again.

As if it were yesterday, I remember my excitement before our first reunion. Since it was to be at our cottage, I baked a chocolate cake, made a hamburger casserole and collected some junk food. Dorothy and Pat brought an assortment of snacks and that was the extent of our planning. We sat at the kitchen table and talked nonstop for two nights and three days. We had one full meal together and after that, whenever anyone was hungry they'd get a slice of cake, warm up a few servings of the casserole or pull out some chips and dip. It was the conversation that intoxicated us.

We were all still married. Dorothy was a High School Math and English teacher and had two sons and a daughter. Pat worked with

Downs syndrome children and raised two daughters and a son while I had four daughters and recently had returned to college.

When one of us had to use the bathroom, conversation was halted so as not to miss a single word. We stayed awake until two-thirty in the morning our first night and almost as late the second. We talked about everything from our experiences with childbirth to our present concerns about our daughters. Within our group of three mothers, one daughter had been traumatized by an assault, two had suffered bulimia or anorexia and one was meeting the challenges of being bipolar. We felt ourselves to be inadequate and yet each of us had tried, in her own way, to help and to heal. Inadequate is not a fair word to use because we did everything we could with the resources we had. Our talk, sometimes so raw with pain, was eased by the support we gave each other and the sure knowledge that all of our children were deeply aware of the unconditional love we have for them.

Politics and religion were kept on a back burner since we discovered vast differences in ideology early on. We all knew that after our initial friendly conflicts, we were probably all so ingrained in our views that to continue trying to convince each other was both amusing and fruitless. We had other things to talk about.

We did recall a Christmas, years ago, when we attended our three churches—first Dorothy's Lutheran Church, then my Methodist Church, followed by midnight mass at Pat's Catholic Church. We laughed as we remembered how some people in town believed the Catholic Church intentionally rang their bells during quiet moments of prayer in the Methodist Church, since they were less than a block away and how the Lutheran pastors daughter called her father Toot. His name was Otto and she was heard to say that backwards or forwards her father's name was the same so she turned his name inside out.

Pat had us in stitches when she talked about their priest attempting to teach his young students what the word miracle meant. "Just imagine," he said in great frustration, "if all the people in our cemetery rose up and walked down Main Street. What would that be?" A young boy, named Oliver, excitedly raised his hand and yelled out, "A PARADE!"

Before our third reunion we invited Dixie, another high school friend, to join us. Dixie had experienced the sudden death of her oldest daughter, Nancy, the year before. Nancy had been attending college at the time and her death came without warning. Our talk that year had a great deal to do with Dixie's incredible pain. When she talked about her daughter, she said it was a way of holding on to her and allowing us to know her. "One of the hardest things is not being able to talk to some people about her," she confided. We cried together, asking questions, hugged Dixie and tried our best to absorb some of her dreadful hurt.

We were astonished by Dixie's courage to become a Hospice volunteer although we were fully aware of how much she had to give to others.

We continue to have a reunion once a month in the autumn and take turns hosting the three-day adventure. We meet in Madison and rent a suite in a hotel within walking distance of the farmers' market on the Square, stay in Spring Green where we attend the American Players outdoor theatre productions or we settle into cottages in either the Eagle River or Hayward areas. We love to do a little shopping and eat lunch at wonderful places, but our favorite hours are those spent over a prolonged breakfast or glasses of wine in the early evening where we catch up with each other's lives over the past year. Our talk can be so frantic in the first hour we're together that one year we each had a limit of five minutes to report on the highlights before we settled down to specifics.

One year I told them about my struggle with clinical depression. Their amazement about what I went through equaled my own puzzlement about what had happened. Before my depression, my overwhelming feeling about my life was gratitude. Then in the fall of one year, I was stricken with an all-encompassing sense of hopelessness. It is in October that we close our cottage and I say farewell to the lake where I swim, sometimes for an hour or more, along the shoreline. It is my spiritual sense of place, my meditation time to think good thoughts and experience creative ideas.

I will probably never know if my depression was caused by seasonal affective disorder, a chemical imbalance or my best guess—

being on estrogen for over thirty years. Whatever the cause, I was blindsided and tossed into a black abyss. My depression was a beast that grabbed me with sharp claws, causing me to feel increased shame and guilt when I could not shake the monster. It seemed the harder I tried to make myself whole, the deeper I became entrenched. I just wanted to hide and lick my wounds and I found it almost impossible to talk to other people about what was happening. I was searching for the light within my soul and my world was black.

I shared with my old friends some of the words I had written in my journal:

Something is happening to me and I'm scared. No, I'm terrified. I don't know if I can put into words what I'm feeling, but I think I have to try. I have to try or I'll lose myself. I feel like I'm spiraling down into a dark place and fragments of me are being torn away as I go down into a cave or a place that I'm not sure I can ever crawl out of.

How terribly sad, how little we really know about each other. I can still play the game and pretend to others that I'm OK. I should have been an actress. How many people are acting?

I want somebody to understand. I want somebody to make me better because I can't. I finally told Dick. He wanted to know why I hadn't told him when it started. Why would I keep something from him? I guess I thought I could make myself better. It was a relief when he knew. I can stop pretending, at least with him. I can at least be honest even if I feel like a complete nothing. I know he's really afraid too. He made me see my doctor and we talked a lot—the three of us. She gave me Paxil. Dick forces me to walk in the country with him. Some days I don't think I can put one foot in front of the other. I just feel like lying on the couch and watching the leaves fall. I even watch some football games with him and I'm sorry when they're over because I have to get off the couch. I don't even like professional football.

Why can't I call my daughters? I just can't. I don't want them to see me this way. Why is it so hard for me to talk to them? I really need them. I sat and stared at the phone for two days and then yesterday I finally called. Each said words that helped me and they said they didn't want to be protected from my pain. This was a big step and it was a good step.

I know that as long as I live, I'll never forget what it's like to be in this cocoon.

I did escape, although it took some weeks. I remember the exact moment. I was lying on the couch in the middle of the night. I'd moved from our bed because I couldn't sleep and thought I'd at least try to read. I couldn't concentrate, of course.

Suddenly, just as the sky was turning red, I sat straight up and knew that either the Paxil had kicked in or I was experiencing a miracle. It was over. Just like that. Hallelujah!

What an incredible relief to talk openly about something I had tried so hard to hide from others. While none of these women had experienced a clinical depression, how strengthening it was to toss aside shame and guilt, and talk to old friends openly and honestly. The Big Four was back in business, now with maturity, humility and a large dollop of compassion.

The College Years

Although I only spent three semesters in college and my friendships were shorter, they, too, left their mark.

During slumber parties, much of our talk focused on boys—finding HIM and sailing off into the sunset. I didn't know a single woman who was bent on a career, although some did get teaching or nursing degrees. Our heads were filled with our individual notions of what our future life would be. That image was a mental photograph of ourselves surrounded by the family that we hoped would be ours.

These friendships were new and consequently much of our talk was superficial, leaving our vulnerable egos intact.

Nancy was my closest friend and I recall a weekend at her parents' lake home in October. We were seven women and had all met at a state college in Wisconsin the previous August. We were sitting on the dock in our sweatshirts and blue jeans, soaking up the remnants of the late afternoon sun, talking about what we wanted our weddings to be like.

Someone said something about wanting their towel colors to be gray and pink, another had chosen her china pattern and a third girl was sobbing over a recently broken relationship. Emotions were close to the surface that day. Our lives during those months were either filled with tragic events, like not being invited to a dance, or wondrous happenings like having HIM ask for a date.

My most vivid memory, on that dock in October, was daring each other to jump, fully clothed, into the freezing lake. I took the dare. I can clearly remember shrieking and then swimming to shore with my water-soaked sweatshirt hanging down to my knees and hearing the other women shouting encouragement.

For the first time in my life I felt truly courageous.

Nancy and I re-connected after years of being apart when I was inspired to call her out of the blue. She was one of the women I reached out to when I experienced depression. The years vanished and we realized that whatever had drawn us together as young college women was as strong and vital as ever.

Perhaps I reached out to her because I needed her to remind me of who I had been. Whatever the reason, she became a lifeline. It was difficult, but essential to reach out to her and more courageous than jumping in a freezing lake.

The Roses

In my fifties, The Roses were born. Again, there were four women. Four seems to be the magic number for me: four daughters, the Big Four, and now the Roses.

This group included Mary, Sue, Jacque and myself. Three of us had duck hunting husbands and that meant we were free for an entire week every October.

Our children were grown, we had some money to spend on ourselves and we made a plan to travel for a whole week every year. Our rules were simple: an interest in playing bridge, an ability to drive a car in unknown places, and a thirst for adventure.

We would take turns driving and the only woman who could give directions was the other woman in the front seat next to the driver who had the maps. The two in the back seat were to offer suggestions for car talk. Wrong turns or getting lost were never occasions for sarcasm or shouting, events we had all experienced when driving with our husbands.

Women, when alone with other women, tend to quickly revert back to days gone by when laughter was close to the surface and smiles were frequent and genuine. There is a euphoria you can feel. Stomach and neck muscles are more relaxed and women can sense the anticipated pleasure of doing exactly what they want to do for a whole week. We were those women and we were giddy with the sheer joy of it all.

We went to Newport, Rhode Island the first year. We knew we could eat whenever we wanted to, even if it was in the middle of the night. We could go in and out of quaint little shops that men seem allergic to and not feel a need to hurry. We could play bridge all morning if we felt like it, wearing our nightgowns and without a dab of makeup. Bliss!

Mary and her husband Tom had rented a timeshare and the apartment in Newport was too glorious for words. Our digs were spacious, beautifully decorated and had a balcony and windows with a superb view of the ocean. We went from room to room, marveling at our great good fortune.

The first thing we did after unpacking was to put money into a common purse and then grocery shop. Lunch was a big affair and we searched out interesting restaurants where we could linger and talk.

That first year we ate at a lovely Victorian inn on a prominent piece of land jutting into the Atlantic Ocean and watched hundreds of magnificent kites fly off the coast on a day bright with sunshine. Some of the kite fliers were having picnics on a lawn so green and lush it reminded us of what it must have been like to live at the turn of the century. It took our breath away.

We visited the summer homes of the rich and famous and were staggered to see mansions along the ocean where families stayed for a mere six weeks in the summer. Some had rooms larger than most living rooms just to store their china and crystal. It seems that "more was better"—a lot more!

After touring the Vanderbilt mansion known as The Breakers, we arrived at the Astor mansion. While viewing one of the upstairs rooms, we found our name. The room was filled with cozy and comfortable seating arrangements with fireplaces against the inside walls. Huge floor to ceiling windows looked out over the ocean where waves were splashing against the breakfront rock wall and in the middle of the vast ceiling was a plaster rose the size of a small gazebo. The docent told us that the room belonged to Mrs. Astor and it was in this room that she visited with her women friends. When we learned that "Anything that was said under the rose, STAYED UNDER THE ROSE," we knew we had found our name. I'll never forget the expressions on the faces of my friends at that moment.

We were The Roses and we could talk about darn near anything, trusting and knowing that our words would stay within our group. We could be vulnerable with each other, a gift I had learned well within the Big Four. We could talk about our hopes, dreams, demons and fears and together build friendships we all knew would last a lifetime.

Every year, for ten years, we planned a trip. The only year we missed was when I had to have surgery that couldn't be postponed. I urged them to invite another woman, but without hesitating, they said if one of us couldn't make the trip, no one would. I awoke from my surgery to find four red roses tied on the bar above my bed.

We whitewater rafted for the first time in Colorado (have you ever had to slip into a wetsuit on a hot day?) and cavorted in the hot springs of a spa. One late evening the four of us went to an outside hot tub. While we were talking, huge snowflakes started pouring from the night sky. It was magical. Suddenly, Mary stood up and throwing her arms skyward, praised the powers that be for sending us such a glorious happening. She smiled and said, "How good it is to be alive!"

We spent a day at Mackinac Island, touring in a horse drawn carriage and then having brunch at the Grand Hotel. Nostalgic feelings surfaced as we could see, in our minds' eyes, women in long white dresses and men in suits and bowler hats strolling across the lawn. How fast time goes! We were reminded, yet again, to make the most of our days and to savor the moments. We stilled time by sitting together on the rocking chairs of the veranda and simply enjoyed our time together.

I remember talking about Mary's Granny doll. She'd found an almost life-size, soft stuffed doll in an antique store. Granny had a gray wool bun for hair and a beatific, if slightly smirky, smile on her face. Since Mary was a saver, Granny had many outfits to choose from depending on the season of the year and Mary's mood. We laughed as we all recalled our favorite Granny outfits—Sue remembering how Granny was dressed to the nines one holiday season with a goblet of wine close at hand. Jacque recalled her in a rather unnatural and impossible pose in a tennis outfit and I talked about finding Granny sprawled out on the living room couch. She was wrapped in a motley old bathrobe, wore fuzzy, pink slippers and had an ice bag on her head. Next to her were a glass of water and a bottle of aspirins. Mary laughed and said, "She spent over a week there and didn't allow anyone to invade her turf."

Sue took us to the home of her friend who was an artist and designed remarkable Santas. We all ordered one, made with special meaning, to delight our families. Sue's Green Bay Packers Santa took the prize.

Our trips continued throughout the 1990s. We kayaked with dolphins off of Edisto Island and in the evening watched hundreds of white egrets return to their trees just yards from our balcony.

One evening while on Padre Island, some years later, we talked about what we really admired and loved about each other. Mary became tearful when it was her turn to be recognized. The three of us talked about her ability to make strong friendships and we all talked about thoughtful things she had done for so many others, ourselves included. I have never known anyone who had as many deep friendships as Mary and without her, The Roses would never have been born. I believe she became tearful because as easy as it was for her to strengthen others, her nature often prevented her from absorbing compliments.

On another trip, we spent a splendid day at Thomas Jefferson's home, Monticello, marveling at his creativity and brilliance. I'll never forget walking around the gardens he had designed so many years before and then gazing at the beautiful Virginia valleys that surrounded his home. Life is so short, we thought. How many days or weeks was he able to look at the views we were looking at? How many views would we look at during our lifetimes?

While in Washington DC, we ran the gamut of emotions.

We spent time in a driving rainstorm at the Vietnam Memorial Wall and the overcast rainy and windy day mirrored our feelings as we saw people leaving notes or flowers below the name of someone who was very important to them. It was a wrenching experience.

Jacque drove our car in Washington DC and we experienced her fearlessness. She informed the rest of us that it was essential to drive aggressively in the big city. Jacque had been an RN and had developed the Infection Control Program at one of our local hospitals. She was used to relaying orders and taking charge. The fact that she had never driven in this particular city was not an issue—for her!

Mary was the navigator and Sue and I were in the back seat, noticing the incredulous looks from some other drivers. Our ride through the late afternoon traffic jams is still a blur to me, while Sue had her eyes shut for most of the trip. To our vast relief, Jacque did just fine!

During this trip we stayed at another timeshare. Mary had called ahead to make sure there was a swimming pool, fully understanding my addiction to water. I chose to swim one morning when my friends were walking, only to find the pool closed. Not one to let a gate hold me back, I walked around the enclosed pool and found an opening. I started to swim, loving to swim in the rain as I did so often at our cottage. Suddenly, a police car roared up to the adjacent parking lot, brakes squealing and tires spinning in the dirt. Out leaped a very short police officer with a Smoky the Bear hat sitting very low on his forehead. I continued swimming. I am fairly tall, with wide shoulders and I've never been able to button a blouse without gaps. The officer walked over to my side of the pool, looked down at me and said,

"Don't you know the pool is closed?" I said we were told that it would be open today. Maintaining his officious posture, he blurted out, "ITS RAINING!" I said something about being from Wisconsin, slowly got out of the pool and hovered over him so that he had to tip his hat to look up at my face. I smiled and slowly gathered my towel and walked back to tell the others.

We've laughed a good deal about that incident over the years. I believe it's an example of a woman's assertiveness that so often does not show itself until later in life. That same officer would have mortified me when I was younger. His over-reaction would have embarrassed my younger self. Now, it was simply funny.

Time moves on and things change. We all seemed to assume our trips would continue long into the future, but that was not to be. The Mary that was so filled with joy in the hot tub was found to have colon cancer. The following October, Sue invited us for a return trip to her lovely home in Palm Desert. We drove from Wisconsin to California, stopping at both Zion and Bryce National Parks. We made our way slowly, allowing Mary plenty of resting time. We had all been to Sue's nine years before on another Roses' trip and had exclaimed over the marvelous desert colors and shadows that were continually changing. Here we were again, with our own shadows lengthening and Mary's life nearly over. It was a bittersweet time, but it was not maudlin.

What do women talk about when one is facing a terminal illness? We talked about the things we had always talked about, in even greater depth and with increased compassion. We talked about our children and our grandchildren and our hopes for them. These talks always brought the most tears and the greatest sadness because we all knew that Mary would not live to see her grandchildren grow into adulthood. I know that she was intensely grateful knowing that her five grandchildren were all thriving and without problems of any significance. She would leave them, knowing that.

We talked about death and our feelings about what there might be after death. I asked Mary, when the two of us were alone, to send me a sign if she could. We agreed that the sign would be an especially distinctive dragonfly, one that might appear as I was swimming around a little island and was, at the same time, thinking of her. That's exactly what happened late last spring. I now believe in some form of life after death.

The following Christmas, during that bittersweet holiday season, Dick and I had a Roses' dinner party with all of Mary's favorite food—pork roast, stuffing, mashed potatoes and gravy—all comfort foods. There were six of us around the table: Mary and Tom, Jacque and Stan and Dick and me. Sue had sent a beautiful bouquet of roses from California for the dinner table, flowers that Mary would take home with her.

Mary's two sons had a special gift for her that Christmas: a certificate for four on the Minnesota Zephyr, a four-hour train ride out of Stillwater, Minnesota. The Roses had always dreamed and talked about one fantastic trip on the Orient Express in Europe.

We decided to dress as we might have had we taken the Orient Express and the following spring we borrowed some wonderful hats with veils and feathers from a local resale shop and dressed to the nines. This was to be our last trip together and Mary was radiant. Some of the other passengers on the train enjoyed our fashion sense and remarked that it must have been a very extraordinary trip for us. It was.

Some weeks after our train trip, Mary's daughter Annie came to spend time with her parents. During their time together, Mary and Annie took a short trip to the southern part of Wisconsin to catalog family pictures and make some family albums. Mary asked if I would drive down and join them for one evening. That evening the three of us spent our time putting together a photo album of the trips the Roses had taken.

The first four pages included photos of the four of us: a childhood photo and one during our teen years, before we were Roses. Spreading all of the photos of our trips out on a large table, we recalled the special things we experienced as Annie decorated the pages with her distinctive artwork. She would ask us what was special about each trip and then record our reminiscences. We recalled playing bridge and bingo on the Ludington ferry on our way to Michigan, our carriage ride in Savannah, Williamsburg, the

Alamo, and the time we ate lobsters at midnight. It was easy to recall the memorable times, even through our tears. We smiled together as Mary remembered what fun it was to lay our shopping purchases out on the bed and exclaim again to each other what marvelous things we had found, taking such pleasure in each other's treasures.

The Roses album was finished, with an old postcard Mary had found for the album cover. It was a postcard with a woman holding a bouquet of roses in her arms. The caption read, "What I know about you!"

The following morning, her daughter Annie and I crawled in bed with Mary and we talked together about her funeral. We listened to her thoughts, and found, yet again, her focus was on other people. I was overwhelmed with emotion upon leaving Mary and her daughter at the end of our time together. One of the things I was thinking about was Annie, when she talked about having a hearth mother. By that she meant a mother who lovingly tended the fires, making her home a place her children and grandchildren always felt cherished. Mary was an exceptional hearth mother.

Mary died in the late summer of 2000. Her final days were ones of astounding courage with her many friends and family members nearby. It would be a familiar sight to see four or five women at her bedside, one rubbing her feet, another arranging pillows for more comfort, while each woman in turn held Mary's hand and spoke her own private words. It was Mary who comforted her friends and I never sensed fear in her.

Mary's funeral was an outpouring of love. In the foyer of the church was a photo of Mary and a vase with four roses. In the reception room, a table held family albums along with the album of the Roses. Her granddaughter, Mary Beth, read a poem she had written for her grandmother called, *Forever Love*. Sue, Jacque and I were among the speakers. Jacque told some funny stories about Mary's sense of humor and recalled a past Halloween when Mary, dressed as a splendid witch, had appeared at her door. Sue, along with her own words, read a passage from *The Red Tent*, by Anita Diament: "I died but I did not leave them. My family stayed beside me and I stayed in their eyes and hearts. For as long as they lived, I walked with them by day; I lay down with them at night. My children moved with my motions; my grandchildren sang the songs I taught them."

I talked about the evening in the hot tub and Mary's joyful spirit. Her legacy to everyone who knew her well was her zest for life.

It won't ever be the same again, although the three of us have some overnights and lunch whenever we can. What we had together however, can never be taken away from us. We have our memories, many too personal to write about. Remember, when we talked, we were "under the rose."

I recently heard about a lovely way to celebrate the memory of cherished friends. Have a lunch in their honor, inviting women who knew them well and spend the time together talking about your individual memories. There will be laughter and tears and perhaps, best of all, each woman may choose to become a bit more like the woman they so admired.

The Lavender Hill Mob

If my husband had not seen a movie from the 1950s with Alex Guiness entitled *The Lavender Hill Mob,* my latest group might have been nameless. In this movie, a group of has-beens had a wonderful adventure. Knowing about our adventuresome experiences, he dubbed us with the name.

Finding each other later in life has been another remarkable happening in my life, and I have my depression to thank for it. As I struggled to escape my cocoon, I literally forced myself to reach out to a few other women. The Roses were wonderful and appeared at my doorstep often announcing we were going somewhere. The somewhere didn't matter. They mattered. We spent the first entire day of my revelation together and there was a goodly amount of hugging and tears. Yet other days were long and fretful. I reached out to Cynthia, a friend from my twenties. Somehow my intuition told me she would be another woman who, because of her personality, might help me overcome the beast. "Let's have dinner together." We did and discovered a remarkable re-connection. My gut sent me in the right direction. Cynthia then introduced me to Yvonne and the chemistry was synergistic.

Yvonne is a poet and she has a keen sense of humor with the added ingredient of encouraging her friends to sometimes laugh at themselves. Putting her collection of old bathing suits to good use, she invited a group of women friends to her summer home, asking them to choose one of the suits that spoke to them. I understand that, had the trying on of suits been videotaped, the shrieks of laughter would have outweighed any embarrassment.

Cynthia opened up her home and hosted an art show and sale for one of her friend's remarkable paintings. Her penchant for enjoying the successes of her friends is without equal.

In her home, she has a Warm Fuzzy Box, and keeps "things that should never be thrown away" in it. Drawings her grandchildren make for her, cards and letters from her friends and darn near anything that, when re-read, cause her to feel both joyful and thankful.

Together we have become increasingly imaginative about how we spend our days together, sensing both a time urgency and a continuing fascination for new experiences.

Both women are truly artists of their own lives and this is reflected in their relationships, their homes, their needlework, their poetry and their spirits.

If you can't laugh at yourself as you approach—dare I call it later middle age?—you might as well throw in the towel.

I have an exercise at the end of this chapter called, "Your Sense of Place," and recently Cynthia and Yvonne combined their ideas on what a nursing home should be. It started when Cynthia said, "I wouldn't mind so much going to a nursing home if we could be there together."

It's important that you realize that, in large part, this is pure fantasy—although an architect might take some notes. Their nursing home would look like a large wheel. The inner circle would be their commons room, large enough to entertain family and friends and invite stimulating speakers to conduct workshops on a grand variety of subjects. There would be a library, piano, kitchen, fireplace and chairs you could sink into (and not get out of?), along with an ongoing puzzle table. The spokes of the wheel would be their own private bedroom spaces and Jack, the cat, would reside with Cynthia. They would have their personal treasures—family photos, music, rocking chairs and books in these spaces and each room would have a skylight on the ceiling so that they could see the stars at night. In between their bedrooms would be a garden space, to garden if they wished or call on a local gardener to mess in the dirt for them. They would each have a small screen porch—with a swing and lots of candles.

Although they'd have kitchen privileges, since Yvonne enjoys cooking and baking, they would have an on-call chef and arm him with their favorite recipes. An accountant too, would be helpful so they wouldn't have to juggle their checkbooks.

Dreaming further, they thought six months in Wisconsin and six months in Arizona would be perfect.

The Lavender Hill Mob has an associate member, Barbara, who is in her late forties. She's officially an associate because she lives some distance from us and is working on her PhD in yet another state while raising four boys. The difference in our ages only makes conversation more exhilarating. Barbara is another spark that ignites others and her creative nature often approaches genius.

When her extended family complained of being tired of circling counters looking for the perfect Christmas gifts, Barbara suggested this playful solution. Everyone in the family should pick another family member's name and when they get the name, they then hear the person's most desired gift—as initials only! The challenge then becomes figuring what the initials might represent within a modest budget. ARC, for example, could mean A Red Car. One of Barbara's sisters asked for TT. She wanted Thin Thighs. She got Twelve Tennis balls. Another sister asked for ABG. She wanted A Baby Girl. She got A Brown Gerbil. One family member, wanting his request to be really difficult, asked for a large variety of initials. He got what he deserved—a can of alphabet soup.

Each time were together—in twos or threes or fours—I feel filled up with creative ideas. An idea might include decorating my home, a gift for a family member, an idea for this book or putting clothes together in a different way. We keep a running list of places we'd like to explore, and, rather than run out of ideas, we live with abundance. Our list is long.

The Sisters' Trips

Understanding the beauty of women together, Dick's Christmas present to our four daughters is money for a sisters' trip. He discovered, years earlier, that a special gift, just from him, gave him a great deal of pleasure. The girls take a trip together about every four years, when their combined gifts allow the planning to begin.

Their first trip found them in Seattle where Anne, our oldest daughter, was living. Her three sisters were all pregnant. Pregnant with babies to be and pregnant with the new experience of the four of them together—to do just as they pleased for four glorious days and until their money ran out.

Another trip took them to Madeline Island on Lake Superior, where they rented a small cottage on the lakeshore. They kayaked around the Apostle Islands, paddling in and out of the caves that exist there and spent one evening soaking in a hotel's hot tub. They did have to climb over a fence to get in but it was early in May and off-season, so no one kicked them out.

Another evening, while making clam chowder, drinking wine and listening to *La Boheme* on a tape player, they made a spontaneous decision. Removing all their clothes and serendipitously—at the height of an aria—they held hands and ran a few feet into the icy waters of the lake where they all dove in.

On hearing this story, I recalled the emotion I felt when I jumped into a lake that October day during a slumber party with my college friends. Was it in their genes?

Their last trip took them to New York City for four days and as I was driving to Madison to meet with the Big Four, they were flying east to meet with each other. I wondered what they would talk about and would their talk be much different from those of us who had graduated from high school fifty years ago. Would they enjoy being in such close contact for four days? They are four very different women and they've had different life experiences and made their own individual choices.

I continue to witness an unbreakable bond between them and that bond brings them even closer as the years pass. I know that these sisters' trips afford them an opportunity, without husbands and children, to come to know each other at an even deeper level. There will be countless times in the future when they will need and depend on each other.

Fate brought us four girls and it's a comfort for me to know each daughter has three sisters, in addition to some lovely women friends, to call upon.

> **Brenda Uleland, a feisty writer and a deeply encouraging woman for other women said, "When we are listened to, it creates us, makes us unfold and expand. Ideas actually begin to grow within us and come to life."**

The following exercises could provide an opportunity for women to listen to other women. These exercises are designed to awaken more of your creative spirit. Remember, when you put thoughts into words, they become real.

Traditional Women and Your Mother

Some characteristics that are common for women, especially those of us at a certain age, are ones that you may have inherited from your mother:

- Wanting and actually thinking that you can fix the lives of others, especially your children.

- A talent for reacting to what's going on around you since you are sensitive to the slightest shift in the moods of others, and the knowledge that emotional highs and lows can leave you feeling like a yo-yo.

- Believing that you are the emotional center for your family so you'd better shape up and meet everyone's expectations.

- Depending on someone else, most notably your husband, for a sense of financial security.

- Having a tough time with anger, with a predisposition to turn it inward, since you are also quick to assume blame or guilt. If you haven't felt guilty about something for a few weeks, you may go out looking for something to feel guilty about.

- Even if you are extremely skilled and competent you will experience more self-doubt than confidence, even in the privacy of your own head.

You might want to take these characteristics one at a time and start talking. What's good or bad about each, in your opinion? How have expectations affected your life? Any you want to get rid of? Can you? It's my belief that attempting to meet the diverse expectations others have for us sometimes bears the added burden of duplicity that injures our souls.

> How about your mother? How many of these traditional women role descriptions were ingrained in her and what, in your opinion, was the result?
>
> Looking at the last characteristic, how important to your psyche is self-talk? What do you say to yourself?

Kate's response to this exercise. She is 47.

"I remember an interesting book I read in college, The Second Shift, *that discussed this epic issue of women being everything to everybody while all the while doing it with flying hair (impeccably coiffed). The book was about social/cultural standards set for women and the impossibility of meeting them without significant personal sacrifice to themselves. The central message focuses on women, expectations and identity that my mother, Joan, encourages us to think about. When she wrote, "It's my belief that attempting to meet the diverse expectations others have for us sometimes bears the added burden of duplicity that injures our souls," I would add that if that is only true sometimes, there are countless other times when the result is empowerment, reward, joy and learning—and that's life!*

"You make your choices and you get all that stuff that accompanies that choice: the good, the bad and the ugly. In terms of how my relationship with my mother affects how I deal with things, I am certainly aware that I have a mental model, or my own subjective understanding of how my mother managed the various challenges she faced. In one sense, I would like to proceed along my journey without the burdens of being overwhelmed, overextended, guilty, etc., but this is an unrealistic condition for most humans—certainly most women. What is most problematic is to not *learn from your own experiences and remain swirling in a vortex of anger, guilt and blame.*

"It's not a simple concept. It's hard to put into words. I think most women understand."

What Do Women Want?

Oh heck, give it a try. Even Freud couldn't answer this one. Make your own list; mine is just to prime the pump.

- To build a strong inner core with enough strength to allow for some emotional risk-taking, creative problem-solving and a continuing exploration of dreams and personal goals.

- To have the courage and good sense to seek our own life rhythm. To follow our instincts about what we value and what is important to us rather than run with the herd.

- To feel beautiful. Not the artificial beauty our culture often dictates, but the beauty that comes from being comfortable with who we are.

- To hear more verbal expressions for our labors of love, be they child rearing, cooking, decorating our homes or building our careers. Grunts don't count.

- To spend more time with people who fill us up, rather than sap our energy. To have at least one close friend who knows us well and loves us unconditionally.

Meg, 40, wrote the following response to my question, *What Do Women Want?*

"Probably, like most minorities, women want it understood that they do not all want the same things, as they would prefer to be defined by their individual natures rather than as a group. Even so, and with full understanding of my limitations as a representative for all of my sex, I imagine that because of our history and our experiences living in female bodies there are some desires which at least many of us do share. I don't know whether these desires are unique to the female sex, but I do know that I hear women wishing aloud for them much more frequently than I hear men. So, I'll take a stab at it, even if it seems to me Freud really was just wasting his time.

"Women want a safe, clean world in which to live.

"Women want access to good health care and enough to eat.

"Women want an inviting, comfortable place to call home—and if this place is shared, a space all of their own within it.

"Women want partners who are fully able to be partners— emotionally, spiritually, intellectually, practically, and in every other conceivable way, or they want to be able to choose not to have a partner.

"Women want to get paid fairly.

"Women want unhealthy, unattainable, unreal standards for feminine beauty to go away and not be replaced by unhealthier, unattainable, unreal standards for feminine beauty as has happened historically.

"Women want time to do what they enjoy. So that they might have this time, they frequently find themselves wanting someone else to notice what kinds of shit work need to be done around them and to do it, without any reminding, prodding, special rewards or enticements."

Color Your Sense of Place

I like this one because it's almost like being back in kindergarten fingerpainting. All you need is a sheet of white paper and a bunch of crayons and some friends because you'll really want to talk about your drawings with each other.

Draw the space you would be the happiest in. It could be a room. What's in that room? Are there windows? If so, what do you see when you look out the windows? What kind of furniture and pictures or photos are on the walls of your room? If not a room, perhaps your sense of place is a garden, a stage in Carnegie Hall, a mountaintop or a place you've only seen in your imagination. What favorite books or music would you have with you?

This is, in Virginia Woolf's words, "a room of your own."

Don't put any people in your space and give your creativity and imagination free rein. Tuck this page away in your journal or in a drawer and take a look at it now and then. You might want to add some things or change your space completely as you age.

Do you have such a space now or is this to be in your future?

Molly's sense of place. She is 39.

"Many, large windows would give her a varied view of natural landscapes, like trees, mountains, ocean etc. She'd like to have a down throw on her big, cozy chair and needs access to books. Music, on occasion, but she prefers the sounds of nature like wind blowing through the trees. She wants a large, wood-burning fireplace. Large enough to walk into and with an unlimited supply of small, dry pieces of wood nearby. She'd like to have some birch logs handy for crackle. On her side table she'd like: fresh flowers (especially tulips), lattes, a bowl of pistachios, red and black licorice and, on occasion, good red wine. She'd like the room to include candlelight and a dimmer switch on the other lights, with a supply of Jane Austin movies without commercials."

Chapter Two

Recharge Your Batteries

> "I had a life with options but frequently lived as if I had none. The sad result of my not having exercised my choices is that my memory of myself is not of the woman I believe I am."
>
> *Liv Ullmann, from* Changing

Liv Ullmann's quote says a great deal about many women. We, who do not know her, see her as a beautiful, accomplished actress and author. Surely she is all of those things, yet she tells us something about herself that reveals regret and astonishing vulnerability.

Variations of her words have been repeated to me hundreds of times as I have listened to women. Why do we, especially as young women, so readily give up choices that are ours to make, either to the idealistic dictates of our culture or the unrealistic expectations others may have for us?

It's almost impossible to pick up a woman's magazine and not read about how we should change ourselves. Our bodies, our hairstyles and make-up, our eating and exercise habits, our relationships, our EVERYTHING!

We must all be a perfect mess. If only we could get a grip on these things, we might be OK. Maybe. Consequently much of our energy is focused on becoming rather than being.

My daughter Kate suggested that I send questionnaires out to as many women as possible in an effort to hear, in their own words, choices they have made and, in many cases, the results of those choices, wisdom that would give other women and something they feel passionate about. Over four hundred women responded, most of whom I will never meet because the questionnaires were duplicated and passed from woman to woman.

I am grateful to these women and find great strength, determination and courage in the parts of their lives they willingly wrote about. I picked a sampling from the returned questionnaires and clustered them according to subject. I give the ages of these women; the words are theirs.

How Might You Use This Chapter?

These words from women could serve as a springboard for discussion with another woman or women. Some of the quotes may result in short chats while others may find you talking far into the night. You might prefer to read them just for your own contemplation. In either case, consider the following questions.

- What do you assume about this particular woman when you read her quote?
- Do you approve of her choice? Do you have any understanding for her decision?
- Do you feel empathy? Anger? What do you feel?
- Is she a kindred spirit or someone you can't identify with?

Can we be compassionate about choices made by women during different stages of their lives and in circumstances different from our own? Listening to the life experiences of other women with an open mind may expose some antiquated myths. Reading the words of women you appear to have little or nothing in common with may help bury old prejudices.

■ ■ ■

These are words that my daughter Meg once wrote to me:

"I don't always agree with you on various topics and life choices, and I don't have a problem with that. I think there is value in disagreement but that a lot of people want to run and hide from conflicting views and I don't get that. Disagreement is about figuring out what you believe. You cannot, or maybe

ought not, hide from yourself. Do all people have a right to their opinions? I guess so, but I think it makes more sense to earn them. Earn them by gathering information, or at the very least, thinking the problem through. For me, just having the opportunity to bounce ideas off, and to sometimes wholeheartedly disagree with my elders, or anyone else, is often an enormous influence on me. I am therefore most influenced by those individuals willing to engage in such dialog, whether they be my elders or itty bitty children."

I think Meg gave us a heck of a roadmap!

Back to the Classroom

"I returned to college at age thirty as a single parent with a one year old. What was most difficult was being the focus of a family inquisition as I struggled to create a vision for my future. Making the transition to better circumstances required a search for answers that were not immediately apparent to me, resulting in intense feelings of vulnerability, failure, guilt, shame and fear. Because timing and circumstances have so much to do with one's success in a learning situation, I approached education with purpose and interest and it made a tremendous difference in many areas of my life: stability, both emotional and financial and relationships with others (son, family and friends) along with my sense of self." Age 47

"Can a mother be a fierce advocate for her child with a disability and still be able to find her own voice? Our third child, Billy, was eighteen months old when he was diagnosed with Down syndrome in the 1950s. With the support of my family I returned to college after twenty years to pursue a career as a special education teacher. Billy and I began our alliance. I relied on him for feedback as I tried new techniques and developed materials, while finding comfort in his company. I also struggled for the freedom to be me since I had a husband and three other children. My son Billy has progressed from a frustrated baby banging his head on the floor to a strong, secure forty-eight year old adult who is respected in the community and vital to the welfare of our family. I recently retired from my career

as a college professor in Special Education. Billy and I continue to speak at conferences. One father wrote to Billy about a comment his young daughter made. 'My parents aren't afraid since they met you.' After authoring or co-authoring six college textbooks, I am writing a personal book about Billy and our family. I am writing about my own strategies for balance because those of us who are pulled in many directions must refill ourselves. I want the world to know that in spite of—or perhaps because of—the pain, the uncertainty, the anger and the frustration of raising Billy, there is boundless joy in seeing him as a happy and successful man. (You may want to write to Jane Schulz if you have questions: 4013 Hemlock Park Dr., Kingsport, TN 37663-2061)

"*My husband was very encouraging and helpful when, together, we made the decision for me to attend law school. Our three youngest children, triplet boys, were eight at the time. Although I regret not getting an earlier start, I'll never regret this choice. My advice to some of my clients is—every day is important. Go back to school. Get independent. Get a life.*" 72

"*I am one of eleven children. After our dad died, we held a family council and found that if we all pooled our money, one among us could go to college. Our choice was our mother. I remember taking over our monthly payments for the refrigerator. My mother became a nurse and financed the education of three of my younger siblings. She's retired now and volunteers with disadvantaged children. Recently she was taken to the hospital with a fractured ankle. She had been teaching one of the children how to skateboard!*" 58

"*Returning to college was the most fruitful choice I've ever made. I've become a clear and critical thinker and now read books and articles expressing many varying points of view. I find differing opinions very stimulating.*" 53

"*I became the first person in my family to get a four year college degree while being a mother with both a full and a part time job.*

Many family members thought I should not have taken the time from my family and that my priorities weren't straight. However I know it was the right choice. I am now divorced and because of my degree I am a successful woman and can support myself and my kids." 42

"Thirty-eight years after I married I earned a lifelong goal by getting my BA. It took thirty years and five colleges." 60

"When I went back to college in my late thirties the quality of my life changed in several ways: I now had an opportunity to enjoy a successful career, I gained personal self-confidence and since I majored in theatre (my passion) as well as communication, I have performed and directed several plays in our community. I have had a great deal of personal fulfillment and enjoyment well beyond career preparation." 66

"Going to college became an obsession for me and was a personal choice that I made. Although I didn't graduate, the quest for knowledge has not faltered for me." 68

Dating

"I wanted to get to know a certain man I met and decided to find out if he had any interest in me and if he had a sense of humor! I wrote him the following note and enclosed a stamped, self-addressed envelope:

> I enjoyed meeting you a few weeks ago at Joanne's party. I'd like to see you again.
>
> Please check whichever boxes apply.
>
> ❏ I'm involved with someone else and she has my complete attention.
>
> ❏ You are too forward. Bug off!

> ❑ I'd enjoy meeting you for coffee or a drink and suggest the following date, time and place.
> _____
>
> ❑ I'm sorry, but I don't remember meeting you. Send a brief resume and photo.
>
> ❑ I've sworn off women!!
>
> ❑ I got a kick out of this note and will call you within a few days. Stay glued to the phone.

"He checked the last box. After several months and a lot of laughs, he sent me a boxes letter asking me to marry him." 45

"When I was twenty-seven I called off an engagement seven weeks before the wedding. It had been a misalliance almost from the start, but I was held in thrall both by the relationship (which was emotionally abusive) and by the fantasy version of our life together, which often seemed more real to me than reality. As the day approached, and the danger signals were flying fast and furious, the little voice inside me started speaking up louder and louder, to a point where it would actually wake me up at night. At that point even my body shut down. I came down with intense nausea and a high fever that even my doctor couldn't diagnose. My finance at the time still relied on me to take care of him! I finally realized that it would be a major act of self-destruction to go through with the marriage. I pulled together the scraps of my self-esteem and called it off. The life I've led since then is a life that would have been unattainable to me had I married him. I now have the courage of my convictions and a much stronger backbone." 38

"The choice I made in 1985 to see a counselor to help me lose weight changed my life completely. I did not lose weight but I met someone in that counselor who knew how to challenge me and set me on a different path. After nine months, he challenged me to date!

He dared me to date two men a month for one year and never date anyone twice. My self-esteem in this area of my life was abysmal. I was forty-one and had had eight dates in my life.

"As I started answering personal ads which asked for someone who was neither young, nor thin, nor pretty, my encounters with (at first) not very desirable, but quickly more desirable men, fueled my self-confidence. I rose to the challenge and dated. Seven years later I married a man I met in a personal ad. Along the way my social skills soared and so did my comfort level in interacting with men." 59

Career

"While working toward degrees in Marketing and Communications, I worked as an intern for two baseball teams, watching for and listening to players for newsworthy items for publication. I believe I made numerous contacts in the sports world, ones that I might use for future employment.

"Before I graduated, I made a tough decision. I decided to work as a nanny for a year so that I could make some money with very little expenses and pay off my college debts. I've always liked being around children and I felt that I needed time to think more precisely about where I wanted to live and how my future career would take shape. I know now that I will never regret my choice." 21

"After fifteen years of being a commercial illustrator, I decided to become a full time studio artist. Emotionally I had to make the choice even when I knew it would mean financial poverty for a time for myself and my children. I wondered so often if a stimulating environment for all of us would compensate for a lack of health insurance and other necessities. I would be living on the edge. It turned out to be the right decision and, in retrospect, I now know that I also gave my children the courage to follow their own dreams." 60

"After leaving both the corporate and academic worlds because I could no longer theorize any longer about injustice, inequality, and climbing the status ladder, I was poor. I sold my blood to the blood bank, swiped toilet paper from public bathrooms and looked for the

barest opportunity to get something for nothing, because my job at an inner city newspaper could not support me. I doubt my capacity for empathy would be as great if I hadn't walked along that edge. Over the last few years I've managed to carve out a living working with and on behalf of low and fixed income people. I think I was brave." 46

"The most significant personal choice I have been faced with, to date, was whether or not to drop out of the workforce and stay home full time upon the birth of my son. Most of my friends worked outside the home and none had chosen to become a parent yet. At the time my choice was not considered socially acceptable and even family members were puzzled, thinking I had made a horrible mistake. My husband, to his credit, was supportive even though my being home meant living on a tight budget and I know he had his doubts as to if we could make it work. In the short term, the results of my decision were mixed—both bad and good. I felt isolated at times, lonely and unstimulated. Anxiety over my decision was a constant. My choice did permit me to meet new friends, those who were home during the day. I had more opportunity to develop a new set of skills and that has value too, like making a comfortable, enriching home for my family. Eventually, my choice led me to a new career path, though that was not on my radar screen initially at all. I am now pursuing my PhD in counseling." 48

"I firmly believe that the point that each person is at their life is a result of all of the choices made every day. I am still undecided as to whether our fates are predetermined (destiny) or if we are able to change the course of our lives by the series of choices we make. I also happen to be the type of person who thrives on change, and sometimes instability as I find it can be a great fix for boredom or life stagnation.

"I have been cooking all my life. Being French by birth and poor by accident, my mother made virtually everything from scratch, from bread to yogurt. I was her kitchen assistant, and by the time I was twelve, could make an entire dinner on my own. After having quite enough of both my bank job and my ex-husband, I decided

to combine my hobby with my career and attend culinary school. Now, after a month long internship with a master pastry chef, I have opened a patisserie.

"My advice to other women is figure out what you love to do—something you could do every day and not get sick of—and then figure out how you can make a living doing just that.

"I would like to do something significant one day that improves the standard of living for an impoverished community. In the past, I worked with teenagers and their families in crisis and found that to be a spiritually rewarding experience until my own health interrupted that career. However, right now I am living my passion." 29

"At age forty I entered the Peace Corps in Zaire Central Africa. After twenty years in the advertising field, I came to my senses and decided to live out my values. My decision took over two years. The results? My choice has changed all aspects of me: physically, spiritually, emotionally and my perspective on what is important in life. I now teach second grade at a Native American school and make less than a fourth of what I made in advertising but my quality of life is superb!" 53

"I was in my early thirties, married and had four kids ranging in age from seven to two. I was working at a treatment center for people with mental illness. I realized that I could probably become a psychologist's assistant or something in the future. Then it hit me: I could BE the psychologist! I decided to go to college and get my degree. So in the past fifteen years or so, I've gotten a BA, MA and am now working on my Ph.D. As I gained confidence, my husband lost his. He was an alcoholic and not around much and things began to deteriorate even from that low point. We divorced fairly amicably and I am now remarried and on the brink of fulfilling my earlier vision." 47

"At age thirty-six, both my kids were going to be in school full time. At this point I could decide to continue teaching, working with my husband or focus on accomplishing the goals in my heart. I had done the other two already and decided this was my time to become an author. It's hard to do something for yourself when it directly affects family finances, who knows if anyone will buy my book and the inevitable question, 'When are you going to get a real job?'" 47

"I believe the most important decision, one that ultimately impacted almost every other area, was my decision to be self-employed. At the time that I decided that I was tired of working at jobs I found tedious and that I wanted to invent my own work, I didn't know another woman who had made such a choice. It was a rather lonely place for a while. But, twenty-five years later, my life is full of other creative self-bossers—most of them women who have followed their own hearts. I also didn't realize that in searching for an alternative to traditional work, I was going to discover ideas that I could share with others who felt the same way. I see that my work has always been about solving a problem, paying attention to what worked, and passing it on." 61

"I guess I feel like we all make choices that affect the quality of our lives every day. But upon reflection, I see that that in itself is a choice. That is, we can choose to make choices or not to. I like to really think and reflect about my choices in life.

"One choice that greatly altered my life was the decision to home school my children. I had already easily decided that life is too short and my children too important to miss out on any part of their life that I didn't have to.

"Because my oldest daughter is blind and therefore has needs not often addressed by traditional schools, I felt my educational choices mattered even more for her. As it turned out, I realized that it wasn't just about picking the best options for my daughter, but about picking the options that make the best use of our family's resources, interests and abilities. How has this worked out with my four children? We have an environment of relative freedom. Our days are our days. On a beautiful day we can go outside and play. We can go to the theatre on a Monday night and sleep in Tuesday morning. School can be anytime, anywhere and often is." 41

"One day at the age of forty-something, I was driving my car and had an attitude change that greatly affected my life! After working as a teacher most of my adult life and always expecting things to change (like maybe my husband would actually be able to make a livable income so that I could stay home with our youngest child), I was struck by the realization that I was a career woman and I could live with that and like it, and be proud of it as well. I would continue to learn more about my profession and about teaching the kids that I had always loved and that would sustain me for years. I suddenly felt stronger and more independent and think it strange that to this day I remember the exact time and place when these thoughts first entered my mind." 69

"When I became 60 I did not run a marathon
Or climb a mountain.
I gardened.
And wrote a book about it
For our grandchildren.
"When I was writing my book, I gained a new and creative sense of purpose that filled the gap I was feeling after retiring from my employment at our local Hospice program. My boundaries were stretched in many and wonderful ways." 62

"In 1993 I decided to leave corporate America to pursue a career as an independent consultant. At that time I knew of no one who had done this so it felt like a huge leap of faith. My husband and I talked through the decision but we really didn't know how this would affect us. He fully supported the move, however, and that made all the difference in the world. We've never regretted my choice. The difficulty of this choice lay in the messages I had grown up with: one career, one corporation, work is everything, the company provides. I was going against everything I had been taught was right. Now those choices seem easy but back then they were terrifying." 48

"Probably my decision to work part time after not working outside the home for over thirteen years. The jury is still out as to *whether it has made the quality of my life better or worse. Personally, I'd say worse because of all my responsibilities. The last person to have quality time is me. I feel good that I'm providing some extra needed money and I do get some personal pride from my accomplishments. However, I don't like how busy our lives are! I was the caretaker, now I'm also a provider. Being a caretaker was already a full time job. If this is what super woman is, I don't want it."* 39

Divorce

"When I made the decision to divorce after twenty-six years, I wasn't angry . . . I was tired! For the duration of my marriage I'd tried to be the woman he wanted. You name it, I did it. I ended up feeling unloved, unworthy and just plain ugly. I was ugly inside because I was angry and this led to depression. When I left he wasn't happy because I wanted to take a pillow, a blanket and a sheet. When he was out of the house, I returned and took only those things my mother and the kids had given me, along with my clothes. I did not take anything we had used together—like dishes. I was angry at the woman I was. A woman who put her own needs in the background and cried for what couldn't be. In time I realized that anger was for the wasted years and living in the past did no good. In short, I grew up." 58

"Divorce. I hate to say it because divorce is such a sad and ugly thing. My marriage was over but I didn't want my kids' parents to be divorced. I also didn't want my kids thinking that what they saw in their parents' marriage was acceptable. And my pride, what would the bridge club think? I regret that I stayed in the marriage as long as I did." 46

"Less than nine years into my first marriage my husband had an opportunity to join a law firm in the small city of my birth, my parents' birth, and my grandparents' birth. The prospect of moving into my family fold was intimidating to me because I was already struggling for self in his strongly ethnic family. Now there would be two traditions for me to wade through. By our twentieth year

our marriage could not survive my sense of need and I marched toward divorce as a lemming to the sea. It was a gesture toward self, which wounded many innocents, but even now, I feel no acceptable alternative." 71

"A choice I made twenty-four years ago changed the direction of my life. I was going through a divorce, feeling rejected and helpless. My lawyer recommended I quit my job, suggesting he could get me more money in the settlement and ongoing child support. I wrestled with the desire to be taken care of, but it didn't feel right. I did the opposite and made the decision to become stronger than ever. I decided to put more energy into my job, which up until now I did to earn an hourly wage. I continued my formal education, joined professional organizations and started associating with professionals. Without fully realizing what I had done, I changed my job into a career that led to opportunities I had never dreamed possible." 62

"For the first time in my life I feel emotionally well. I'm a better mother without all the tension I've lived with and I know that I am capable for the first time in my life. I didn't want my daughter to think being submissive or dependent was normal or healthy. I've recovered my sense of humor." 48

"Like almost everything else in life, there is a down side. My divorce has upset my children's lives to a degree I never thought possible and I've suffered tremendous financial setbacks." 43

"I had to stop thinking he'd return and that took a long time." 61

"Following my divorce, I suffered surprising losses with people I thought were my friends." 35

"It was a good thing that nobody asked me for a date during the six months following my divorce as I might have married the first man that came along. My life has been a series of abandonments, first my birth mother, then my adopted mother, my first husband

and finally, my daughter-in-law. These issues have greatly governed how I feel about myself. When you're happy with yourself, and this took me quite awhile, then you can form a genuine and lasting relationship." 66

"My husband walked out on me, leaving me to raise our eighteen-month-old daughter alone. I had just resigned my teaching job so that I could spend more time with him and our child. We lived six hundred miles away from both of our families and I felt very isolated. Both my husband and an attorney said I wasn't allowed to leave the state. After a lot of red tape, I sold belongings and moved back home where my daughter was nurtured by grandparents, aunts and uncles on both sides of the family. She grew up without seeing a lot of her dad, but knew what the love and security from extended family members means." 52

"I chose to leave an abusive relationship. It was the hardest thing in the world for me to leave a man who had convinced me I was nothing without him, but I'm alive and well now without him." 27

"By age twenty-one, after my husband sought a divorce I was suddenly the single mother of three. There weren't many of us around in the early 1960s. Choosing, when I was fifty-four, to raise my own four–year–old grandson, when his mother, my eldest daughter, became involved and married an ex-con drug addict was a life changer and he enriched my life unbelievably. What a treat it became for me to raise this child with the wisdom of maturity and a purse that's a little more full." 62

"At twenty-nine, I was faced with a life altering decision. I chose to no longer live with my abusive husband. I had three young children that deserved to have a better life than living day to day with anger, alcoholism and betrayal. I was terrified and had no means of support. It was the lowest point of my life, but some amazing things began to happen. I had to go back to work. We lived in a trailer in a rural area and I didn't have a car.

"The phone rang after two weeks of terrible anxiety. It was a friend of my mother's offering me, at no charge, her ten-year-old car. She said she was getting a new car and they wouldn't give her much for a trade-in. Now, at the age of sixty-two, my career is mentoring women." 62

Emotional and Physical Health

"I made a choice about not holding resentments from my past. A person I know has a way of bursting my balloon when I'm at my most joyful. It took me a long time before I realized that her hurtful remarks said everything about her and zero about me. Why is it that some people see relationships as a seesaw? If they can knock the other person down, they can somehow lift themselves up! I hope you will tell other women about this because I suffered too long for nothing." 39

"Deciding to stay home with my four children, rather than pursue a career was an emotional upheaval for me. It has brought joy, a great loss of self and some hard years." 44

"When our daughter died, her death hit us very hard. She was forty-five. Musically talented, she played the guitar and sang. Nothing could stop the inexorable decline of her stage four breast cancer, yet she made a final CD the last year of her life while laying flat on her back. For two years following her death I could not bear to turn the calendar to the month of her birth because her absence was so overwhelming. Then a friend who had also suffered the loss of a grown child showed me a way to cope with my yearly agony. Instead of trying—and failing—to ignore her birthday, we planned a celebration of her life. Family and friends were invited to a pot luck supper. We spoke of her and wept when we needed to. We watched a video of her final concert and I even bought her a lovely birthday card. Instead of a great lump of denial, I felt in touch and as though I could breathe through the day and evening and survive. This year I plan to have an even bigger party." 74

"Choosing to be a yoga practitioner has greatly improved the quality of my life. It wasn't a difficult decision and it's obvious that I feel better and more grounded now. I'm also able to live much more in the moment and with that has come a great sense of freedom." 24

"I want to warn other women about spending time with someone, under the guise of friendship, who can deplete your energy and leave you drained. Some years ago a woman I liked started camping out at my home. She talked insistently about her problems and I was the listening board. She even followed me into my bathroom once, still complaining about her life. Sometimes, when I had a multitude of things to do, I literally felt like she was clinging to my legs as I attempted to ease her out the door. My son was in grade school at the time. Years later, he told me that his heart fell whenever he saw this woman's car parked in our driveway as he was walking home from school. He knew I wouldn't have time for him. I felt worse than terrible. Beware of such women." 55

"When I look at the choices I have made during my life, the one that always surfaces was my acknowledgement to myself that I am a lesbian. I had felt for years that I was slowly dying of sadness. Once I admitted my sexuality, my life improved greatly and I became motivated to be productive in my work and enjoy my life." 53

"Ten years ago I started an affair that lasted almost that long. I thought at the time that everything revolved around this man. My self-esteem was shot and towards the end I didn't like myself much at all. I wish I'd never become involved with him and I pray my kids never find out. The fact that I would lose their respect will haunt me until the day I die. I would never recommend this to anyone, because it seldom pans out. I have a black hole in my heart." 49

"My choice, originating with a kitchen disaster and ended up causing my friend and myself a darn good laugh. One Christmas, expecting a house full of guests, I had spent time, cooking, baking and freezing. Everything was going to be perfect, and that meant

making a special scone recipe for a brunch. I was in a hurry, since my friend and I decided we'd reward ourselves to a movie two days before company came. I misread the recipe, adding one cup of maple syrup to the mix instead of one-half cup. Believing I could save the day, I kept on adding flour, sugar—whatever. Putting this mess of dough on the cutting board and then trying to cut diamond shapes turned into a homemaking catastrophe, but being nothing if not one-track minded, I baked a batch. The final insult was when globs stuck to the bottom of the cookie sheet. In frustration, I threw everything in the garbage, but I could not get the idea of having scones for brunch out of my head. I told my friend what I'd done, following the movie. I soon realized why she was so empathetic. She had planned a pork roast with all the trimmings for her family meal until her daughter said (plaintively), I thought we were going to have a Norwegian dinner. My friend said she was going back to the drawing board and planned to make homemade lefsa that night! We started laughing so hard that we were convinced passerbys thought we were both hysterically crying. My choice is to stop taking myself so seriously, laugh more and bake less." 64

"My decision evolved, it didn't happen overnight. The choice I made was to be more responsible to and for myself. Being more honest about my decisions and their consequences. I ask myself, 'Am I being proactive or reactive and if so, why?' Even though I frequently struggle with this, it does get easier. It's very liberating to know that you really do have a choice of how to live your life." 60

"The best choice I ever made was to attend meetings of Adult Children of Alcoholics. I had an opportunity to review my past, forgive my parents and really start working on my own needs. The end result helped me to end the cycle of abuse in my family." 43

"After my husband's death it would have been so easy to fold, give up and throw in the towel. A wise woman had the courage to ask me to be the woman the father of my children would want me to be. In spite of my anger with her for not being more sensitive to my

pain, I am grateful my intellect listened to her counsel. The welfare of my young children was more important than the misery and pain I wallowed in. I did have a choice and am so thankful for the decision I made thirty-three years ago." 80

Joy!

"*My mother initiated this escapade when I was a young girl. Sundays were our day. My father had died and mother worked the other six days of the week. We'd get into her Model T on Sunday and explore, often with a picnic lunch or the expectation of a newfound roadside cafe. I remember the afternoon she suggested we take every road to the left. How we giggled that day! We picked flowers in the summer, gathered leaves in the fall and pine boughs in the winter. Decorating our home with the things we found extended our fun and I felt so close to her during those times. She was so encouraging about my creative efforts!*

"*After Mother died and I married, my husband and I continued this tradition. Every month or so we took turns planning an adventure for the two of us trying to surprise each other and only told the other what to wear. We did this for years and had so much fun together—from theatre events to lunch at a country tavern. If I had the choice, I'd do it all over again.*" 93

"*I'm an only child and when I moved across the country from my parents' home, I wanted to do something memorable with them before I left. My folks are great, but were all pretty closed mouthed about our feelings. After thinking about it, I gave them both a short list of four questions and asked that they each pick one that we could do together. These were my challenges:*

1) *Take me to a place where you were the happiest and tell me why you felt that way.*
2) *Take me out to lunch and tell me a family secret.*
3) *Take me to a place you've never been.*
4) *Spend some time with me looking over old family photos and tell me some stories about our relatives.*

"Mom took me to a park and told me she'd come there with me when I was a baby. She told me about the other young mothers she met, what they talked about and how happy she was then. One of the women she met in the park is still her closest friend.

"I can't believe what Dad did because he's such a conservative man! He said he thought about my questions a lot and decided to take me to the one place in our community he'd never been—the adult bookstore! I've never laughed so hard with Dad as when the owner said something that led us to think that I was my father's young floozie! We still laugh about that day." 37

"My choice was to light a fire under my husband! We'd talked about a trip to Hawaii for years but it never got off the ground. Idea! I rented a hotel room for one night and asked that he meet me there. When he came, looking really puzzled, I was dressed in a sarong and had tropical drinks and macadamia nuts on the coffee table. I also had our calendar, travel brochures and flight schedules. Well, it was a dandy evening and we did go to Hawaii three months later!" 58

"At the age of forty-two, I found myself somewhat restless. I'm not exactly sure why. I had a good marriage, three great kids and a solid career. My life was full and yet I searched for something more! The something more became a beautiful boy from Siberia who we adopted. At fourteen months he was extremely deprived on all levels and it took three years of intense focus, treatment and patience to provide the security he lacked. There were many days when I questioned my choice because the stress caused by a needy child does take its toll on everyone in the family. Slowly things began to improve and just recently when I saw him triumphantly mounting the steps of the school bus, blowing kisses at me through the window and waving just like all the other kids, I felt fulfilled! It wasn't an easy route, but by far, the most gratifying choice of my life and I know my family has done something both meaningful and significant. We've all benefited!" 49

"As a wife and mother it seems that every decision was made around my husband and children. When my last child started first grade, I decided to take flying lessons. Didn't ask, didn't tell anyone! It was such a life changing decision for me and it took guts and perseverance to swim against the tide and prove that I could do it. Being a pilot has made such a difference in my life." 51

"My choice is to manufacture fun and bring a laugh to others. My younger sister made a big deal out of my turning fifty a few years ago, sending me a package of Depends, hair rinse, support stockings and arthritic medications. After reading the poem, 'When I am an Old Woman I Will Wear Purple,' and nine months before her big birthday, I asked my friends to search for anything purple, gaudy and cheap! They rose to the occasion and every few weeks I mailed a package off to my sister. Purple underwear (used and found at a thrift sale), a purple feather boa (the feathers were molting), a ring with a huge purple stone (plastic) and a purple umbrella with fringe (found at a flea market) were among the finds. On her actual birthday I sent her a stunning red hat that might have embarrassed Mae West." 54

"Know that you can change choices you have made that aren't working for you. Life goes by quickly and before you know it, you're middle-aged and wishing you had concentrated more on enjoying what each stage of your life had to offer. Make sure you continue to do something or learn something that defines you as an individual. This is especially true if you're a stay-at-home mom. For example, I didn't take dance lessons as a child although I was always fascinated by tap dancing. At age forty, I signed up for a beginner's class and got hooked. I still dance and even perform on occasion." 66

"I have always worked around horses. I was offered a position with a very good polo player when I was nineteen. I didn't feel qualified and I had twenty-four hours to make up my mind. I said yes and those were six of the most wonderful years of my life: traveling and training polo ponies." 52

"When I was eight I contracted polio and spinal meningitis and spent a year in an isolation hospital before going to a convalescent

hospital. Being paralyzed on my left side and from the neck down on my right side, I was told I'd never walk again.

"I told my mother I was going to walk regardless of what the doctors were telling me and she said that I could do anything I set my mind to. On her next visit she brought me the most beautiful pair of red shoes I'd ever seen and red is my favorite color. She set them on my bedside table so that I could look at them as much as I liked. A girl in the bed next to mine, with polio said it was silly to think we might walk someday. She is living her life in a wheelchair and though it took me a long time, I did walk in my lovely red shoes." 61

"I am fifty-five years old now. Five years ago I fell madly in love with a man fifteen years younger than I. We had so much in common and I've never been more fulfilled in my life. At first my family and friends were happy for me, until they became aware of the difference in our ages. Then all I heard were comments like, 'Whatever will his parents think? Will he still be around when you're sixty? Have you thought about how embarrassed your children will feel?' Their well-meaning remarks caused me to do some serious introspection, but love won out.

"One day I bought some helium balloons and a bottle of wine. I selected a crystal goblet from my cupboard and took a black magic marker and an old blanket. I went out into the country and chose a spot where no one would see this weird woman. I lay the blanket down, poured some wine and wrote on each balloon a negative comment someone had made. One by one I let those suckers catch the wind and fly off in space. I married him and I have never regretted my decision." 55

"Wanting to do something both unique and fun for my ten-year-old daughter's last birthday, I asked her girlfriends to come to the party dressed as what they wanted to be when they grew up. One of her friends came with an assortment of dolls: she wanted to be a mother. Another came in a homemade nurse's uniform with a big red cross sewn on her white tee shirt. I was tickled when my own daughter asked to wear a safari outfit. She wanted to be an explorer and see the world!" 32

One of my favorite stories about zestful women comes from an experience I had on a shuttle on my way to an airport. It was an ungodly hour in the morning and facing a long day ahead I resolved not to talk to anyone, to just cozy down in my seat and look like I was sleeping. That worked fine for a while and then the shuttle stopped at a small town and a woman, somewhere in her seventies, got on and sat next to me. I was still pretending slumber until I heard her say to herself, "I could howl with joy!" My eyes snapped open and I asked her if I'd heard her correctly. She assured me I had. She then told me her story. She was on her way to meet her daughter and granddaughter at the airport and they were flying to Greece together for three glorious weeks. She told me about her daughter being a breast cancer survivor and that a trip the three of them had planned two years previously had to be cancelled because of her daughter's surgery. She was so excited that the two of us talked fast and furiously for the next sixty miles. I was on my way to do a Zestful Women! workshop and she had given me my opening words. I hope the three generations of women had a spectacular time!

■ ■ ■

Are you struck, as I am, with the continued importance, throughout our lifetimes, to ask ourselves, "Is this what I want my life to be like?" Your gut will give you answers, your intimate friends can help, but the ultimate responsibility is yours alone.

I must now look at my rear view mirror to answer the question about choice. I'll return to a time, thirty-five years ago when I was thirty-four years old.

My wish is that I might be a Gretchen Grimm for some of you. She was one of the women who helped me jump some hurdles in my life.

When the youngest of my four daughters started kindergarten, I went back to college. I had completed three semesters before I left school, married and moved to Madison where Dick was a senior. I literally went from a college where I was much involved in both theatre and debate to a job counting coupons in a grocery store in Madison, a job that helped a little with our spartan lifestyle, but didn't do a thing for my diminishing sense of self. My relationship with Dick however was wonderful and our decision to marry when we were both twenty years old proved to be inspired!

I believe that I made the decision to return to college when I was thirty-five years old because I began looking at the lives of women several years older than myself and I knew that I wanted to fill future years with much the same joy that I witnessed in women who were doing exciting things in their lives. At the time I didn't have a clue as to what exciting things I would aim at, but further education seemed a good start.

I started with one class. A week or so before classes started that fall, I timed how long it would take me to get to the class and I remember standing in the empty classroom deciding where I would be comfortable sitting and wondering what on earth the following months would bring. I didn't know anyone who had returned to college in their mid-thirties so I had no touchstone. This was in the late 1960s.

Time passed and my initial apprehension and anxiety evolved into feelings of enthusiasm and a growing sense of confidence. These feelings, however, took some time to move inside of me and take a firm hold. I was far too busy doing. I remember that I tried so hard to be everything to everybody, proving to others that I could still maintain my home and do all the things I'd done before while still finding time to study. Finding time to study had eluded me completely in my first college attempt over fifteen years before.

I often felt pangs of guilt about leaving my daughters with other people while attending classes. It has always been interesting for me to observe, in myself and other women, how quick we are to embrace guilt.

My mother was my greatest supporter and Dick became increasingly encouraging when he realized that this was not a lark, but a growing commitment to myself. He did, however, wake me up in the middle of one night, absolutely furious. Through tight lips he told me about his nightmare where I, of course, was the culprit!

We were on a big ship together with our four girls. (The closest we'd come to a big ship at that time was a rowboat.) We were all on the deck of the ship and the sea was stormy and raging. He was walking ahead of me talking to another man. I was behind with our daughters. In his nightmare, I was not paying any attention to the girls and seemed to be in my own world. Warning me to watch them, I paid no attention to him. Suddenly the storm caused the deck we were walking on to tilt dramatically, and, one by one, he watched our daughters slide into the sea.

It is frightening and many times upsetting when your partner changes course. Most of us are victims of wanting the known to continue, especially if it's been a good known. When one in the marriage ventures in a new direction, fears that we never knew we had can surface. Well, Hamlet said it better! We survived and the girls were all at the breakfast table the next morning and I went back to my classes.

My greatest surprise was the reaction I got from a few women I'd always thought of as friends and I was confused with their subtle sabotage. I write about this because I've heard several other women who have made mid-course corrections or ventured out in new directions tell me about similar experiences. Sometimes we have to go it alone for a time. It can be confusing and hurtful because what we generally feel, when we are in the early stage of a new choice, is insecurity and anxiety. It was my experience to go through a reshuffling period over a few years. I held fast to the friends that were true and basically flushed the few whose toxic response to me was pulling me down out of my life. This was a time, between the Big Four and The Roses and, as many women in their thirties know, quality time with women friends has to be fought for.

Not all of my college courses were fun. Early on, I found I had to take a dreadful Statistics class to fulfill a requirement for a Psychology major. I tearfully pleaded with my adviser to allow me to take two other courses replacing the wretched one. No soap.

I walked into the Statistics class only to find students, who like me, wished they were anyplace but there. The professor appeared to be suffering from hemorrhoids. He never smiled. He simply walked over to the blackboard and drew a upside down curve. He turned and said, "Do you all know what this is?" I didn't have any idea and no one answered. He continued, "This is a normal curve and this is how I grade." He drew four even vertical lines within the curve. "A few of you will earn As. An equal number will fail. Some of you will earn Bs and an equal number Ds. Since many of you are average, you will earn Cs."

Well I knew which category I'd fall in!

I sweated through that semester and felt the weight of the world was lifted off my shoulders on the last day of class. I've seldom felt such relief. I was wrong about which category I'd fall in and I know what got me through the course was telling myself before an exam, "I'll just remember this dumb stuff long enough to take the test and then I'll get it out of my head."

I did graduate with degrees in Psychology and Speech. Along the way some darn fool asked me what I was going to be after graduation. Now, in addition to college courses, I had to BE something! After some thought and very few options, I set my sights towards teaching. Yet another hole in my future was plugged.

I know many women who have returned to the classroom, many who have pursued masters and doctorates and several who have done so in their fifties, sixties and seventies. Not a one of them has ever spoken to me about regrets and their struggles and triumphs would make for inspiring reading.

My advice as I look out of my rear view mirror is: find yourself a mentor—a woman or man who will lead you through what can sometimes feel like a mine field. There was a professor, Jim, who kept me from stepping on a mine and with his encouragement pushed me forward. Now thirty years later, I have been invited into his classroom to speak. His entire focus for the semester is encouraging his students to reach for a higher quality of life by questioning, reading and Socratic discussion.

You might make a connection with another woman who has completed what you are beginning—someone who will rejoice with you as you successfully persevere and who both fills up your tank and lifts you up.

Here are some exercises that might be enlightening for you as you go about your own decision-making. I know that they have helped me at various stages of my life.

Yes, No and Wow!

What have you said yes to lately?

What have you said no to?

When have you last felt WOW!?

When have you recently felt excited about something?

Here's how Jane, 41, responds to this exercise:

"I've said yes to too many things: an eighth grade recognition party, a post prom party and a church brunch for five hundred people.

"I might say no to my husband's request that his ninety-six year old grandmother come to live at our home. I wonder who would be taking care of her?

"I'll be feeling WOW after I finish drawing the plans for a spec home that will be built this spring. In addition to the plans, it will be up to me to find, hire and manage all the work that needs doing."

Vision Folders

As you're paging through magazines, clip out photos, slogans, phrases or words that appeal to you. They might have to do with short term goals you've set, decorating your home, fashions, ideas for your garden, holiday decorations, scenes from places you'd like to visit, nutritional advice or darn near anything that catches your eye. Pay close attention to pictures that have a strong emotional appeal to you. Keep collecting until you have several clippings to choose from.

Then, perhaps on a rainy afternoon, bring them out and look

The Big Four
(Standing, from left: Dorothy Wheeler and Dixie Fixmer. Seated: Joan and Pat Branigan)

The Roses
(from left, Mary, Sue, Jacque and Joan)

The Roses' last trip on the Minnesota Zephyr
(from left: Joan, Jacque, Sue and Mary)

The Lavender Hill Mob at afternoon tea
(from left: Yvonne Brunstad, Cynthia Larson and Joan)

Joan's Daughters in New York City
(from left: Molly Button, Anne Charnley (standing), Meg Sirianni and Kate Fleming)

Facials and Wine
(from left: Kate, Meg, Molly and Anne)

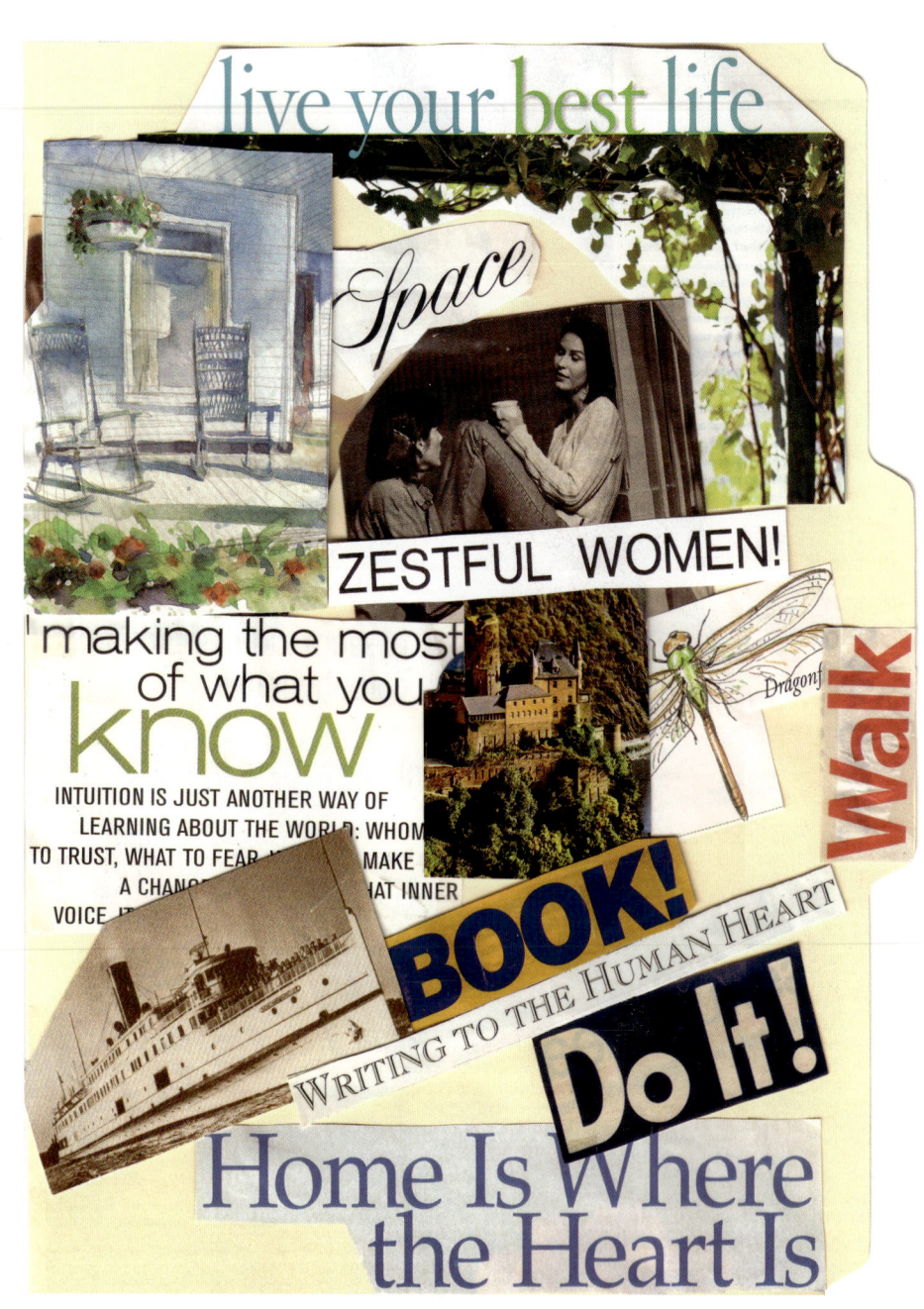

A Page from Joan's Vision Folder

them over again. Have a plain manila folder, scotch tape, a few colored pencils and glue handy.

Make a collage on the four sides of your folder. Choose from your clippings things you would like to include or make happen in your life. Cut and paste, adding words of encouragement to yourself when appropriate.

You now have some visions for your future.

After a time you will find that at least some of the things you've included in your folder will actually come to be. It's kind of like programming your gut for future happenings.

I've done vision folders for quite some time and the results have astonished me. About six years ago, one of my vision folders contained a picture of a ship. I had had a vision for some time about sitting in one of those marvelous deck chairs, looking out at the ocean but felt it to be an unrealistic expectation. A few years after I'd made this folder, Dick and I were taking a walk out in the country. I don't know what possessed us since it was a cold and blustery day in January. As the wind blew into our faces, freezing our faces and causing our noses to run, we decided to check on the Internet for some greatly discounted trips on cruise ships. We found one and learned this would be the last trip this ship would ever make since it would soon be put into dry dock. It was far from any notion you might have of a modern cruise ship! It had been the SS France and when I saw it for the first time, it was as close as possible to the ship in my folder. Go figure.

Vision folders can certainly be a solitary exercise, but the fun of talking to a friend or friends who have done the same thing can give you further insights into your dreams as you ask each other questions and spur each other on.

> ### *Looking at Your Accomplishments*
>
> This exercise can be a great self-confidence boost and may help you if you're wrestling with a difficult choice. Take a blank sheet of paper and draw two vertical, straight lines so that you have three columns to write in. Divide your present age into three equal portions and write those ages at the top of the three columns. For example, if you are sixty, your first column would be birth–twenty, your second column, twenty–forty and your third forty–sixty. In each of the three columns write three things that you feel very good about accomplishing.
>
> Digest them if you're alone. Talk about them with a friend or friend who has done this same exercise.

Anne, 48, wrote her responses to this exercise.

Birth–16 yrs.
1) *I walked when I was eight months old—eager to get around, I guess.*
2) *Piano lessons and my friendship with Minnie, my feisty 76-year-old piano teacher.*
3) *My growing awareness of how important nature and animals would be throughout my life.*

Ages 17–33
1) *Creating adult relationships with my three sisters, who, over the years, have become my closest friends.*
2) *Taking the risk to attend nursing school when I knew I'd be one of the oldest students in class.*
3) *Taking an even bigger risk and moving across the country to begin a new career as an RN at a Veterans Hospital in Seattle. I was exhilarated and scared to death at the same time.*

Ages 33–48
1) *Marriage to a man from a different culture and finding him to be kind, loving and supportive.*
2) *Increased understanding of the woman my mother really is.*
3) *Finding my own voice and sense of self. Now I'm working on listening to it.*

We're going to drive along now. I think you'll be as astounded and encouraged by the wisdom of other women as I was. Fasten your seat belt!

Chapter Three
Every Car Should Have a Compass

> "If you have knowledge, let others light their candles in it."
>
> *Margaret Fuller*

A few years ago, while visiting with a group of about nine women, a daughter of one of the women joined our group and, after some time, asked the rest of us for some words of wisdom. She had been living through a difficult time in her life and was experiencing both indecision and doubt, unhappy about some previous choices and unsure of present one. We leaped in, and wanting to help, spoke almost as one voice.

- Become an emotional risk taker.
- Dare to do things that fearful people don't attempt.
- Dream big.
- Be expressive with your love.
- Don't waste time wondering what other people think because other people are usually wrapped up in their own lives and aren't thinking about you at all.
- Design your own life with passion and gusto.

I was able to follow her progress for a time and she did indeed make some life-changing, gutsy decisions. I think she would have made these decisions in any event, but it sure can help to get that extra boost from caring, more experienced women.

That discussion propelled me to ask women the following in my questionnaire: What wisdom would you pass on to younger women?

I was captivated when I read their words and have chosen another sampling that represents many of the women who responded. I've

Philosophical Wisdom

"I've found, in my eighty years of living, that in most situations only two choices or solutions are available. Give in, give out, quit OR go on and we don't need to muddy the waters with counseling. Many people shrink from audaciousness, deeming it frivolous and not of substance. All wisdom is not found in peace and quiet. Volumes are hidden in aggression and malaise created by passion. I'm eighty on my birth certificate but I believe I am fifty and will be fifty-one in March. Delusional? Of course, but it works for me. I spend time trying to convince this place I reside in—my body—to cooperate. Most days, I succeed, with the help of my jars and stuff that comes in bottles from the drug store.

"My waltz through this life is pleasurable and I am so grateful to God for it. I love what I do—owning a woman's clothing shop where I meet so many interesting people and hear parts of their life stories." 80 (50)

"I remember hearing this quote from a clinician at work. 'There are only three things that I need each day I wake up: someone to love, something to do and something to hope for.'" 48

"Try to refrain from making judgments about other people's choices. When I was a young bride, I was often critical of my mother-in-law's choices. I was unable to see how her decisions were based on her background, her experience and the values of her generation . . . not mine." 57

"Don't give up being yourself for a man. The only person you need to please is yourself. Don't be controlled by a boyfriend or husband. I see this happening so often with young women that I want to scream, 'Don't allow this!' But, I guess, I was a young woman who did the same thing." 70

"Forget the words 'blame' and 'possess.' 65

"Always be sure a room has an inviting place to read a book. My daughter once said that when she walks into someone's house for the first time and doesn't see a cozy place to sit and read, it's not a home. She also said she grew up in a home, the nicest compliment she could have given me." 68

"What would I say if someone asked me to write down some words of wisdom? At 61 they would be different from what I would have written when I was younger. At this age there is a sense of urgency about living to the fullest. One of my greatest concerns at this age is that I will settle. That I will seek comfort over purpose— that I will go along and get along and thereby deny my passion. There is a concern that I am going to miss it, whatever it is. I do not want to seek a long life at the expense of missing a full life. I want to be wide open to life. Just like in the morning I always quickly open the shades—may I open my heart and life to what is out there. Not so open that I do not weigh things and consider their implication, but open to LIFE.
"As I get older, I am stiffer in body parts, but am quicker to love and listen and slower to speak. May people want to be around me, but may I be content when alone. I know that a life of passion and abandonment is risky and can carry the possibility of being labeled crazy or fanatical, but the risk is worth it. I often ask myself if passion and peace can co-exist. For me there is peace in passion. Settling causes me more unrest in the long run. Status quo is not for me. One time when I was really passionate about something, someone said to me, 'Calm down, Elaine, it's no big thing.' It was a big thing to me and I hope that I never calm down if it means abandoning who I am. I also recognize that this passion I am talking about is not something I can drum up myself. It comes from a source that is greater than I. It is a gift. I will stop writing now but will not stop loving, seeking, pursuing and living with expectancy until I draw my last breath." 61

"Kill your TV. Don't read stupid magazines intended to cause you to hate yourself and thus spend countless dollars on fashion, make-up and self-mutilation. Play hard. Work hard. Question experts. If you must get married, marry someone who is a good cook. Get to know yourself really well. Practice saying, 'That's bullshit and I love that,' and do what you love. Don't pick your nose in public." 41

"Every other person alive has or has had his/her own struggles. My struggle is unique only in that it is mine! Don't fear sharing and looking for connection. Every human being has something to teach us, whether by word, act or simply quiet example. Look for the lesson and respect the source." 71

"The dishwasher is an invention I regret. I have had some of my most rewarding discussions with both my daughter and sister-in-law while standing at a sink while one is washing and the other, drying dishes. Quilters have much the same experience I believe; while hands are busy, honest feelings are often shared." 68

"Trust your intuition, your gut feeling. We all have that inner wisdom and just need to listen. When you're feeling discomfort, take time to figure out what that feeling really means. When you go against your intuitive sense, inevitably there will be struggles." 47

"Young women don't realize how strong and resilient they are. They look to the outside for strength when all the strength they need is within." 86

"Happiness is the successful balance between letting go of expectations and understanding one's own needs. Remaining open to life as it is instead of imposing an idea of what it should be allows process and innovation. Trust the process!" 45

"Don't always give others the benefit of a doubt and then doubt yourself!" 48

"In my experience the happiest people are those who simply follow their passions and incorporate what they love into their lives." 15

"Be an explorer right from the start, not so you can get it out of your system, but so you can develop a lifetime of curiosity, learning, passion and growth. Give yourself as many experiences as possible and pay attention to those that make you happy!" 60

"I would urge young women to get their education before pursing any other goals or desires. It is, in my opinion, the best way to build self-esteem because one need not ever be financially dependent on another person." 57

"I've never been happier since I was finally able to step back, take a leap of faith and let things happen. Now I try to let things unfold in their own time. I don't try to figure out the path beforehand. Oh, believe me the fire is still there and I'm hard of hearing when I hear the word no. But I've learned that the answers come from the most surprising places, the unknown reveals itself in its own time, and the end result is better than I could have dreamed." 60

"If you call a spade a spade, be prepared. Know that very often people would rather call it something else. If it's important enough, persist. Don't join the ranks of people who choose to look the other way, shove it under the carpet or sugar coat it until you can't tell it's actually a spade." 52

"My mom said that every twenty years, a person's life changes. That got me through three kids in cloth diapers and their high school years." 61

"The world is composed of boys and girls and men and women. Women are grown-up girls with children. Boys are no good until they are grown up and married. My Dad is so nice that I think he must have been a girl when he was a boy." 8

"People don't so much remember the words you say to them as the feelings they have when they're around you. You can either live with abundance or scarcity, believing that there's enough out there for all of us or you'd better get your piece of the pie before someone else takes it away from you." 49

"I will try to measure out an inch and a half of wisdom in the space provided! There is an unfortunate hormonal/biological predisposition to hurl ourselves into partnerships or marriages at a time when we are least capable of making logical, rational and well-informed decisions about the rest of our lives. This is exacerbated by a kind of mob mentality, where, phenomenally, everyone seems to be doing it. I did it myself and I see high school girls doing this routinely and predictably. My wisdom is: DON'T DO THIS!
"Learn about things, yourself included. Pay attention and ask about the experiences of others so that you might learn from them." 47

"Please slow down! You have more important things to achieve than housework. You can never get the years back to when your children were young and your parents were still alive." 77

"There are certain virtues that I wish I would have had when I was younger. Among them, patience to wait, to anticipate and to plan more carefully and prudently. During the initial time of the Woman's Liberation Movement, few of us had time contemplate, deliberate or think. We felt like we had to seize the moment—NOW.
"Perhaps understanding how these decisions might have influenced the lives of people I love, I might have slowed my determination to reach the pinnacle of my career.
"Lastly, I believe gentleness is the key to the good life. We must think and act non-violently. We must focus on humaneness first and foremost. I believe that the only significant way to build one's self-image, to interface with family and friends, and to deal with people, is to be loving, caring and openhearted (not weak). Life is not an easy road and everyone needs all the loving care we can muster. Women hold the life keys to gentleness, nurturing and wisdom." 65

"Everyone else is more concerned with the way they look than the way you look. In other words, be comfortable in your own skin and do what makes you feel good." 39

"If you listen carefully to the voices inside you and respect your intuition, you won't fear the criticism you might hear from the outside voices." 61

"Don't allow the limited perceptions of others to define who you are. There are people with toxic behavior all around us who just love to see someone else fail. I guess it makes them feel better about themselves." 56

"I've come to believe that when a woman thinks she is superior to others, she must constantly ignore or diminish the talents she clearly sees in other women." 72

"My wisdom is that to keep growing a woman must be able to discard some old beliefs and attitudes to make room for greater compassion and sensitivity." 81

"Women should remember that an unhurried sense of time is a form of wealth and necessary for spiritual growth." 79

"I think its my tendency to, sort of like Dr. Frankenstein, borrow certain aspects of another person's wisdom and leave others behind. My mentor or role model would be a composite human built by my own imagination. There was a philosophy teacher I used to really admire in college, but I was afraid of her. There is a Unitarian minister somewhere out there, Gretchen, whose sermons always touched a spot of truth for me and I have a feeling she'd have been a fine mentor for me in some ways, but I got sick of going to church. Come to think of it, she did too." 41

"Even though I'd known my future husband for a long time, since our parents were friends, I wasn't prepared for his depression. I was

aware of his mood swings, and my naive nature told me he would outgrow them and that my joyful self would lift him.

"We raised our family in good order; my husband's mood swings didn't deter our family time. Things changed after the children left the nest and we moved to a new location. It was OK borrowing the money for the house, but it was too much to handle borrowing money for unexpected renovations. Something snapped, and from then on he has remained in varying degrees of depression.

"I wasn't accustomed to surroundings with a depressed person, especially the part about having to be most careful not to set off the next episode. Any treatment for him was out of the question. So the problem went on for years, and my usual happy self was being dragged down with him. I began to have feelings of resentment and anger. I didn't like what I'd become and had to do something before both of us became worse.

"I was fortunate to have a basic enjoyment about everything and everybody so it was frightening to lose myself for quite a while. I wanted my husband back—the man who used to sing along with the greats on the radio, frivolously dancing from room to room with my feather duster. The man who would find lovely surprises in the most mundane things.

"How could I return to my serene world? The first painful thing I did was to partly let go of the good man I loved. Truly, I alone could not help him. When a problem came up, I'd do what I could for him, but was determined not to let his problems get to me. A blessed result happened from my new vantage: I was able to be more empathic and understanding toward him.

"By not letting him get to me, I have been able to save the core of me. I cherish the essence of me that allows me to be free to dance, sing, rejoice over our children and grandchildren, to create, appreciate and to pursue what my life was intended to be." 68

"At age forty-three, when our three children were in middle school, college and one just married, I learned I had breast cancer. I had so much to live for! My dad had died of cancer many years earlier when he was just fifty-three and I thought I too would die.

"Following surgery my pastor visited me and it is his words of wisdom that still brings tears to my eyes almost twenty-four years later. He said, 'Trouble makes you bitter or better and the choice is up to you.' My experience with cancer triggered me to rethink my priorities in every aspect of my life and, without question, I've become a better human being." 67

Wisdom about Relationships

There must be a zillion different reasons for relationships to either crumble or flourish but I think you may find some wise words from others.

"Never become involved with someone who is married or in a committed relationship. You will never be able to fully trust that person and you might end up not liking yourself." 46

"Be sure you understand what kind of man you are committing to before you get married. Open your eyes and take a good look at his family. Don't discount genetics." 44

"Find mentors in all sectors of your life: work, family, creative, spiritual and emotional. These mentors are people you will intentionally choose because you admire and respect them. They will give you a roadmap from which you can make your own high-quality choices." 48

"Build traditions and rituals within your families. I kept a journal about my granddaughter beginning the day she was born. I'd write in it whenever I had something to say about her. I marveled at her accomplishments, commented on her inner beauty and growth and kept programs from her dance recitals and other memorabilia along with family photos within the journal. When she was fourteen, we read the journal (she for the first time) together and I was very touched as I saw what my writings meant to her." 67

"Get involved with a multi-generational group of women and listen. The stuff you will learn! In my experience the older women smiled a lot at the younger women and remembered how it was for them when they fell in love, married and raised their families. They are the keepers of the stories and the rest of us learned what's healthy and what isn't and when to worry and when to let go. We confront each other, comfort each other and cheer each other on." 46

"Don't take your mother for granted. When you're a teenager your mother may seem like she doesn't understand you or nags you all the time. It may seem like her rules are old-fashioned and, I know when this is happening, it feels awful. However, as time passes, you will realize how much you love her and what a void there would be in your life when she is gone. It's at that time that you'll wish for just one more lecture from your mom." 32

"Take the time to learn from your older relatives, your family history and their stories. If you wait until you have time it may be too late." 62

"When you are married and feel like you'd like to throw in the towel, this is normal. Work at being better at loving." 89

"The role modeling of your mother may be second nature to you, but remember that you probably tuned into her fears as well. By getting to know and listen to other women, you will have many more choices as to how to live your life." 41

"When your children are young and most especially, teenagers, encourage them to talk to one of your trusted friends about things they can't open up to you about. They may find relief and be open to some good advice they'd close their ears to if you said the very same thing. The catch is that your friend cannot report back to you and this must be honored." 69

"Let people change. I've had the opportunity to watch many of my siblings and friends in their professional roles and I am impressed. My older sister would be my nurse of choice if I were ever sick. She's cool under pressure, concerned, but not overly so, and not grossed out by anything! I've seen her in action and been able to look at her as a grown-up. Otherwise I'd probably keep replaying her in my mind as that dipstick Merry Sunshine who used to jump on my bed in the morning and sing to me." 46

"When it was time to celebrate my husband's birthday the first year we were married, I decorated the house with balloons and made several posters wishing him a great day. His remark? 'Wouldn't one poster have been enough?' My wisdom is to concentrate on making your children's birthdays a day for them to remember and make one poster for your husband's natal day." 39

"Don't get married expecting your husband to support your personal goals and ignore your weaknesses. That kind of happily ever after only happens in fairy tales." 70

"Always have some money of your own so that you won't have to be accountable to someone else for every nickel you spend. The amount doesn't matter nearly as much as the control you might allow the other person to have. I'm writing about dignity here." 77

Personal Motivation

"Something I do at the beginning of every new year is work on what I call my value deck. I make a list of between ten and twenty values or priorities that will be important to me in the coming year. I write each on a 3 × 5 card, also including a little something about it. Each year I shuffle the cards according to their importance, adding some and changing others. This simple exercise raises my awareness." 62

"On a superficial note, you know how we women are so self critical about our physical appearance? Have you ever looked back *at photos of yourself at seventeen, twenty-seven or whatever and thought, "Jeez, I looked pretty good back then, " when back then you didn't think so? Listen more to your heart and gut and less to your head."* 49

"I've been relishing my own identity ever since I finally discovered it—somewhere in my late fifties." 75

"Drink lots of water and learn to breathe deeply." 48

"Escape the ordinary and be your own woman. Dress with your personal flair even if you have to sort through Goodwill to find things. My own experience there has been to find some terrific buys. Money is far less important than good taste and good taste means your taste!" 46

Wisdom. Its a difficult subject for me to get my thoughts around. Is wisdom a one size fits all? I doubt it. Is wisdom the result of experience and age? I don't think so because I've seen a goodly amount in young children. Can we become wiser by learning from some of the mistakes others have sensibly offered? Well, that's always been a tough nut to crack! One of my mentors—although I will never meet her in this world—was a woman of great insight and profound wisdom. That woman is Anne Morrow Lindbergh. I've read her journals and, of course her lovely book, *Gift from the Sea*. She writes:

"Woman must come of age by herself—she must find her true center alone. As I talked with women, young and old, with different lives and experiences—those who were hard working housewives and mothers, those who wished careers, those who supported themselves and those with more ease—I found that my point of view was not unique. In varying settings and under different forms, I discovered that many women, and men, too, were hungry to discuss and argue and hammer out possible answers. Even those whose lives appeared to be ticking imperturbably, under their smiling, clock faces were often trying, like me, to evolve another rhythm with more creative pauses in it, more adjustment to their individual needs, and new and more alive relationships to themselves as well as others."

So, perhaps, we are not meant to grab a hunk of wisdom, become complacent, and sail through life. Anne's wisdom reinforces my own belief that we have opportunities for growth every day and that those of us, who are willing to discuss, argue and hammer out life's challenges can become increasingly more reflective and aware.

Some of the best wisdom, in the form of advice, I've ever received came from Gretchen Grimm. Gretchen was an art teacher at our local University and was one of the most imaginative women I've ever met. She occasionally invited men and women from our community to come to her parlor (not living room) for lively conversation, many times inviting people she had simply heard about.

It was there that our relationship began and I became aware of her thirst for new experiences. "I'd like to try something new at least once a week!" was her motto. The something new could have been anything from building a stone birdbath in her back yard to writing a romance novel.

Over time she became my mentor, although mentor was never mentioned, just friend. After leading one of my first workshops that I knew was a mild disaster, I sought her out. Entering her home and feeling akin to Pitiful Pearl, I said something like, "I think there must be thousands of other women in Eau Claire who could design a better workshop."

Instead of saying sweet nothings that I wouldn't have believed anyway, she fixed me with her steely eyes and said, "But you're doing it! Now, what about the workshop should we talk about?"

I will never forget her words because they left room for a personal sense of failure while replacing much of my agony with a huge dollop of better things to come.

It has been comforting, over the years, to remember her words and, in a very real sense, she gave me permission to fall flat on my face sometimes—as long as I got up and tried again!

For any reader who is attempting a new direction in your life,

I give you Gretchen's words, "You're doing it! Now what would you like to talk about?" Find a mentor or trusted friend and start talking!

Another slice of wisdom comes from my mother. She has been dead for over thirty years and yet she enters my mind every single day. I learned how important laughter is from her and I learned to distinguish the important from the unimportant. Years ago when my now forty-nine year old daughter was two years old, Mother and I were having a heart to heart conversation at the kitchen table. Anne grabbed a glass of water from the counter and proceeded to dump the contents on the floor. As I lurched forward to clean up the mess, Mother grabbed my arm and said, "Leave it. It will evaporate. Let's keep talking."

My wisdom? It isn't mine since I believe it to be the foundation of all the world's religions, but it is nevertheless, what my response would be. My father often expressed his love to my mother, but he never said the words , "I love you," to his three children, although his actions spoke volumes. Like my father, I often had difficulty expressing what I was feeling.

My wisdom is to become very good at expressing your feelings—all of your feelings. Those you love will be loved more completely. Others will better understand you and you won't have a bunch of old garbage in your gut to get past. Stuffed feelings never die you know; they just have a habit of coming out in uglier ways. In turn, you'll undoubtedly become a more nutritious person for others in ways that might surprise you—like becoming one of a rare breed, a good listener.

After I graduated from college, I taught part time at our local technical school. After teaching Psychology classes for a few years, I had an opportunity in 1974 to teach a brand new class—Assertiveness.

My first Assertiveness class held over thirty students. The room was filled with young men and women, around the ages of 18, 19 and 20. The class was exhilarating for me because I learned some effective communication skills at the same time that I was teaching them to my students.

One day in class, toward the middle of the semester, two students started asking why it's so hard for so many people to express loving feelings. I heard comments like:

"Do you really have to say the words?"

"Aren't a person's actions more trustworthy?"

"Are people embarrassed?"

"My mom says it but my dad doesn't."

"I say it to my dog!"

Suddenly the classroom was a hailstorm of well insulated points of view and I realized, yet again, how many of the young men and women were carrying emotional baggage, pain and unresolved issues—almost always from their families of origin.

Spontaneously (and because it felt right), I gave them the following assignment:

"Tell your parents that you love them. If you don't feel love for them, forget the assignment and no questions will be asked. If you have open expressions of love in your home, I'd urge you to tell your parents, individually, something you admire and respect about them. No phone calls. No letters. I'm asking you to have a face-to-face conversation and I'll give you three weeks to complete the assignment." I circled a date on the calendar and told them that all of our discussion that day would be about their experiences with their parents.

The circled day came and I walked into the classroom that afternoon trying to still my own anxiety. Had I trespassed on a subject too intimate to disclose to others? I felt it would be difficult to re-create the emotions in the classroom that were now three weeks in the past. I was surprised to find that the classroom was full, no absent students, and yet the air was tense and the classroom unusually quiet except for a few whisperings. Many of the students didn't look or smile at me.

I had promised myself to just let things develop and to let the students define the class. I would not fill the empty spaces with my words.

There were a good many tears and wet eyes in the classroom that hour and some of the tears were mine. Only three students out of thirty talked about open expressions of love in their families and those had come from grandparents.

A young man, known for his comic relief, announced that he couldn't do the assignment until he'd had a few beers. Returning home from a bar after midnight, he found both of his parents in bed with their door closed. He opened the door and yelled, "I LOVE YOU BOTH" and then fled to his own room. His dad groggily followed his son, asking what that was all about. The class was only told, that "We had a brief conversation of substance." This was said with a straight face.

A rather quiet young woman, Susan, who always sat in the back of the room, tentatively raised her hand. I have never forgotten her story and these are very close to the words she used:

"I live alone with my mother. My dad died when I was small. I don't remember him at all. I love my mother and I know she loves me back, but we haven't said any loving words to each other for months.

"I can't seem to please her and if I had some money, I'd move out in a minute. I know she's tired from work and all but we never have any decent time together. I'd rather be with my friends. I know she's angry too but why do I have to feel like she's angry with me?

"When I signed up for this class, I promised myself I'd do all the assignments because I know I need this. When you gave us this one, I didn't see how I could and I knew you'd let us off the hook.

"I've been thinking about this assignment every single day and it's kept me awake some nights too. Anyway, I did it last night. We ate supper and Mom went into the living room to watch TV. I stayed in the kitchen trying to get my courage up and then I walked into the living room, asking her to turn off the TV because I wanted to say something. She turned the volume down and I walked over to the couch and sat next to her like a zombie. I was shaking like I'm shaking now. I said something like, 'Mom, we haven't been getting along all that well lately, but I just wanted you to know that I really do love you.'

"I guess I expected her to say she loved me back, or give me a hug or something. She didn't say a word as she turned the volume up on the program she was watching. After what seemed like a *long time, but was only seconds of uncomfortable nothing, I went to my bedroom. You don't want to know what I thought of your assignment!*

"*I got up later this morning because I didn't want to see her before she left for work. As I walked through the kitchen to grab something to eat (at this point in her story she was crying and reached to the floor to get what appeared to be a large roll of white paper which she asked the boy next to her to help unroll) this is what I found in the kitchen. My mother made a banner out of this freezer wrap and taped it to the cupboards.*

"*The banner said, I LOVE YOU SUSAN in letters a foot high.*"

I have no idea what went through the minds of my quieter students that day, what touched their hearts or what choices they would make in the future except for one amazing coincidence. Last winter we knew it was time to have our fireplace flue cleaned. Dick called a man to do this chore. When Steve had finished, I invited him to have a cup of coffee and shortly into our time together he looked at me and said we had met before—almost thirty years before. He'd been in one of my Assertiveness classes. Steve talked about some of his memories from that class, remarking that the one that has stayed with him the most profoundly was the love exercise.

An additional piece of wisdom comes as a result of an experience I had when I made the choice to leave teaching and find out if I could build a career presenting workshops. Having made my choice, I went to the head of my department asking to talk to him. He had hired me six years before to teach Psychology and Assertiveness Training. I told him that I had appreciated the opportunities he gave me but that it was time for me to move on. As I started to talk about my ideas for workshops, he lurched across his desk and pointing a finger in my face said, "You will fail. And when you fail don't come crawling back to me looking for classes to teach!"

I left his office shaken and unsure of my decision and frightened to death about burning my bridges behind me. A tentative leap into self-direction was quickly replaced by a slide back into self-doubt. That is such a familiar feeling for me that it's like an old friend, a friend with ugly warts. My tank was almost on empty that day.

Months later I asked myself how I could even consider allowing someone who really had no idea of who I was or what was important to me, to derail me. Fortunately, the seeds of my future had been planted and it would take far more than this person to pull them out by the roots.

I write about this because I've witnessed too many occasions when a woman has attempted to reach for a goal and someone has put an emotional roadblock in her way. The great sadness is when the woman listens to such foolishness and never realizes what might have been.

I encourage everyone to listen to their own heart and their intuition. This is important even when dealing with as serious a subject as depression. I regret to say that, before my own experience, I was among the insensitive uninformed.

It hurts to write that because I know now what an incredible difference the responses of other people can make. They cannot provide the cure, but they can keep a troubled person from feeling so dreadfully alone. Feeling isolated and then isolating yourself from others is a critical issue. Guilt and shame should have nothing to do with a person suffering depression. They do however, for many of us, because our medical knowledge is not yet up to speed and humans, being human, may even think it's catching. Genetically it probably is.

I was talking to a woman not long ago and she told me about having coffee with two other women when, out of the blue, an old college friend rang her doorbell. In the course of their conversation, the college friend asked if, by chance, anyone had any Paxil. She had forgotten hers and didn't want to be without it even for a few days. Two of the women reached for Paxil in their purses and the third was up and on her way to her medicine cabinet.

If you have a friend that is suffering, one of the most loving things you can do is pick up the phone and let them know you care. If you live close by, pick up the phone and tell them you'd like to drive over to their home and just sit and talk or get in their car and get out of Dodge for a few hours. You can provide a safe place for them to try and put into words what they're experiencing, as long as you both know that whatever is said "stays under the rose."

Don't ever hesitate to check in with them after the depression is under control, asking how they're doing and what they might need that you could provide. If you are tentative about using the word depression, don't be because it can cause the person to believe it is shameful.

If you are suffering, talk to a doctor and those closest to you. Don't try, as I did, to think you could somehow conquer this through sheer personal strength. My doctor told me that believing you have an ability to control often deepens the depression.

Dick and I have had several talks about what the suffering person can do, along with the medication, to help themselves. Walking is one thing, even when you don't think you can get off the couch and walking with someone who cares might give you twice the benefit.

Don't hide—even when that is what you yearn to do. Reach out to a few people who you know instinctively will be on your side and tell your truths. In many cases I believe good friends and loving family members are more beneficial than educated counselors. In addition to understanding, they bring love.

I'm not a Pollyanna and yet I look upon my depression now as a gift. I discovered some new friends, rediscovered some old friends, and deepened my relationship with Dick and our daughters and now am a more compassionate woman. I like myself better.

Toni Morrison said, "Whatever you have that's worth keeping, pass it on." I did.

> ## How About a Few More Exercises?
>
> Here are more questions to ponder—alone or in discussion with friends.
>
> Have you been loved enough?
>
> What qualities do you seek in your friends?
>
> What is the most important thing you learned when you read the chapter on wisdom?
>
> Whom do you admire and why?
>
> Who is the most memorable character in your family?
>
> What dumb things have people said to you that for a while, you believed?

The last question is one I write about in my journals when I find that comments from people I care about turn out to have a poisonous aspect and are flung in my direction. Often wearing the mask of concern, their words can hurt as I repeat them in my head. When I am able to stand back and give my sensitivity the fresh air of perspective, I realize their words were saying far more about themselves than they were about me. This has always been a healing thing for me to do and often stops my defensive remarks in their tracks, leaving my self-esteem intact.

Yvonne, 75 writes about the most memorable woman she has known:

> *"Ruth is a lively and agile eighty-two year old woman. She really knows how to play and to be with her is to have fun. She enjoys writing and among her offerings is a book that takes place in the fictitious town of Farrenwide entitled,* The Chili Jamboree. *It concerns a chili contest where the tickets to vote for a favorite recipe will help support a new fire station. There are sixteen entries, among them Sister Mary Overwork, Orly Oppenglosh and Edith Transmitter. Edith Transmitter is six feet tall and flat chested. She listens in on other people's phone calls down at the telephone company where she works. She's a good soul though and probably*

lonely. Edith has never been farther from home than her Uncle Acney's chicken farm but she always carries this enormous brown pocketbook and in it is a toothbrush, a change of underwear and a map of the USA just in case. When it comes to cooking, Edith doesn't know beans and has been known to bring Jell-O® to the church picnic. When we got her chili recipe we figured she got it over the phone when she was listening in. So, if this happens to be your recipe would you please let us know?

"*Ruth loves her home and decided every room in it needed a gift. Among the gifts was a set of ivory satin sheets for her bedroom. She nursed her husband until his death from cancer and one of her five children was severely disabled. I remember her saying, 'I could still hold him and carry him when he was seventeen years old.' Among the things Ruth has done to maintain her strength was to join forces with five other women and create their studio—a building where they can retreat to both work on their art and validate each others lives.*"

Mentoring and Role Models

Mentoring relationships between a younger and an older woman can be very nutritious for both. Having a role model can expand our vision of what we might become.

Other than your mother, who would you choose as a role model and why?

This person can be dead or alive, known or unknown to you.

Who have you (or are you) mentoring and what is (or was) your experience? What did you talk about? What was your purpose or focus?

> ### Master Dream Lists
>
> Creating a master dream list means keeping and writing down experiences you'd like to have during your lifetime. You might break your list down into the following categories:
>
> What you'd like to learn or learn more about.
>
> Where you'd enjoy traveling.
>
> Things you'll really consider to improve your physical and emotional health.
>
> What is your passion?

My sister Ruth, 65, responds to, "What do you want to learn or learn more about?"

"I can never learn enough about animals and nature. Animals never cease to amaze me and I've learned so much from them. I read once that when you go to heaven, every animal you've ever loved runs to greet you.

"I'd really like to learn to be more tolerant of some other people, especially those that don't share my values and I want to learn to be less concerned with the day to day chores so that I can learn to tap dance."

I admire Ruth. She adopted two dogs from humane shelters and after training them to be therapy dogs, takes them into hospitals and nursing homes, brightening the days of many people who are missing their own beloved pets. Harvey, one of her big dogs, can often be found right up on the bed with a resident or patient.

Ruth married a widower with three grown children and six grandchildren when she was in her fifties. Upon discovering boxes of family photos and memorabilia in his home, she made six remarkable albums for each grandchild, bringing to life their family roots.

I encourage you, whether alone or with others, to write your thoughts down before talking. Writing is a process that can unlock both creative thoughts and feelings.

We're going to take some side trips now as I write about some unique and glorious groups of women I'm either familiar with or have heard about.

I'm calling these groups *Spark Plugs*.

Chapter Four
Spark Plugs

> "However deep our devotion may be to parents or to children, it is our contemporaries alone with whom understanding is instinctive and entire."
>
> *Vera Brittain*

It would be unusual to find a woman who has not experienced a gathering of women. The Red Hatters have become the most visible group and outfitted in their red hats and purple clothing, their zest for life is contagious. These are women who have found the company of other energetic women to be one of the best antidotes for advancing years.

But ask many other women about their more personal experiences and you will hear about some very diverse and imaginative groups. Women have always banded together for there is strength to be found, ideas to be shared and dreams to be recognized. The women's wagons circle when one of their members is in distress and they bring much more than a casserole or a cake with them in times of the greatest need.

These are some groups I am familiar with and the uniting factors appear to be common interests and skills, a capacity for innovative experiences and a boundless gift for laughter.

The Stitch and Bitch Women

These women, as countless women before them, come together to quilt. One member told me she restores her soul with the rhythm of the needle and thread. The lives of these women are as interwoven as their stitches are and each daughter and granddaughter of the nine women has been given a unique quilt made collectively by the group. Their ages vary as daughters and daughters-in-law have recently joined the original members and when I asked them to tell me something about their conversations, I heard the following story from a great grandmother with a sparkle in her eye:

"My choice was to start using my good white towels! A little background: my mother taught me to always save my good linen and towels for company and that's just what I did for fifty-six years. Then two things happened: my eighteen-year-old grandson came for a visit and my house burned down. On the morning of the fire, my grandson came into the kitchen with ONE OF MY GOOD WHITE TOWELS SLUNG AROUND HIS NECK! I gave him holy hell since he was family not company. He looked at me as if I'd lost my mind and later that day, after my home burned, the only thing that escaped was the white towel hung on the clothesline to dry. My priorities changed in a flash. What are we saving things for?"

A younger woman and single mother to four boys told about her choice not to fall to pieces when her old station wagon was stolen. Instead, she gave herself a Pity Party! She sent invitations to her quilting friends saying they would drink cheap w(h)ine, listen to sappy country music and compare irrational belief systems. Some of the women even brought her bouquets of dead flowers and they had a grand time. She finished by saying that, "It's hard to stay depressed when you have friends like that!"

This same woman said something that made me leap for a pencil and paper: Truth is in the throat and trust is in the gut. To get to your heart you have to go either way."

The Gourmet Group

The Gourmet Group meets in restaurants to discuss women's literature. Their idea of gourmet food is eating out and the food always takes a backseat to the stimulating conversation. As one young mother of three who is one of the group's founding members said, "I was standing popping popcorn for a school event and I got to thinking that I could probably do more with my life! I wanted to talk to other women about their thoughts on feminism. I've been confused and torn, motivated and thrilled by books written by women about their experiences and I needed the thoughts of other women who have read the same books to sort out my own values and beliefs."

This group evolved to include women of all ages and they talked passionately to me about one of their discussions. They had asked each other what wisdom they would pass onto younger women and here are some samples of their responses:

"Figure out what you're good at early on and capitalize on that. I'm good at getting people enthused."

"My friend Paula is a good listener. My other friend, Jody is a good problem solver. I learned that when I'm feeling down, I must first talk to Paula and THEN Jody because she'll begin solving the problem before I'm done with my emotional workout!"

Another woman told the group about a walk she had taken with her eleven-year-old grandson and his dog Daffy.

"Daffy ate like a goat—anything and everything. Imagine my embarrassment when Daffy threw up a mixture of unidentifiable vomit in front of my neighbor's house! I was flustered until my grandson made me laugh when he said, 'No big deal, he just barfs and gets on with it.' Now, when life gets the best of me, I tell myself to just barf and get on with it!"

The Eat and Argue Group

This group of accomplished and risk-taking women also enjoys good food but their focus is on hammering out subjects that usually cause discomfort and conflict. Each meeting a different subject is selected by the hostess, ranging from abortion to the latest political battle. Every woman is assigned a position to uphold and defend—the twist being that their given position will not reflect their current beliefs. It's very important that the women listen to each other, without interruptions, until the discussion is opened to the group at large. Not surprisingly, once firm positions have been modified, understanding of another's viewpoint is increasingly respected. The women have found that there are always many more questions than rigid points-of-view as their discussions progress.

Perhaps their most humorous discussion came when the subject was, "Is it sometimes advisable to tell little white lies or must one always speak the truth?" Not surprisingly, both sides offered well thought out reasons to support their positions and an *I Love Lucy* program was recalled when Lucille Ball was challenged to tell nothing but the truth to her women friends for one entire day. Lucy failed.

The Women's Adventure Club

This group was formed when six career women decided they needed more spontaneous fun in their lives. The original group of seven set these guidelines:

1. We will all take turns planning an adventure. Adventures should be an experience out of the ordinary and participatory rather than passive.

2. Try to keep the cost of the adventure under $25.00. (This is not an absolute, since overnights are acceptable.)

3. Information to be included in a flyer the planner sends prior to the adventure:

    Don't say what the adventure is, although hints and clues would be fun

    Date and time span

    Meeting place and directions

    Clothing needs

    RSVP information

    Cost

    Relevant information, like bringing a sack lunch (Include phone number for husbands or baby sitters; no fair calling ahead to see where the adventure is!)

4. Send your fliers out at least three weeks before the adventure you are planning.
5. RSVP is important
6. We are going to establish an adventure scrapbook. Bring a camera.
7. Be creative and fun loving! ONLY WOMEN WITH GOOD SPIRITS ALLOWED!

This group has grown, thrived and changed over the years. Adventures have included a tap dancing lesson, Tai Chi, vegetable sculpturing, mime, karate, elocution, kayaking, voice lessons, skateboarding and ballroom dancing. They get together for parties a few times a year and a recent event was a party where the single women in the group, now numbering twelve, invited their ex-boyfriends or ex-husbands for the other single women to meet. I was told it was an evening of high anxiety and, perhaps for good cause, no sparks were ignited!

The Woman's Retreat and Food Fest

A woman's retreat has been held for over fifteen years at a Northern Wisconsin lake. The hub of the wheel is Kathy and the spokes might be her sisters, daughters, high school friends, bosom buddies or a fascinating woman she met the week before. It's an informal weekend gathering and the women come and go as they please. Everyone brings food and drink, maybe a book they believe they will have time to read, and sometimes, a sleeping bag if they know they'll arrive after all the beds have been taken.

Some years have seen a more formal structure, as in this excerpt from an invitation in the early 1990s:

There will be a talent night as part of our pageant to select the Goddess of the Lake. As part of the pageant, contestants will entertain us with their talents, readings, songs, dances, jokes, etc. There will be NO swimsuit competition, and a costume of your choice depicting a famous woman will take the place of the evening gown event. Make us laugh, or cry or think! Yes, we will have that most precious segment, THE QUESTION.

There are, in fact, several questions. (Some asked as part of the pageant, and others responded to around a late night campfire) A sampling:

> There is a theory that we marry our parents. Which one of yours did you marry and why do you feel this way?
>
> Is there a person from your past you would like to see and talk to again? What would you talk about?
>
> Has your life been what you expected it would be? Why or why not?
>
> Who is your best therapist (yourself, spouse, female friend)?
>
> Who had the greatest positive influence in your life?
>
> Who had the strongest negative influence?
>
> Describe yourself in four words.
>
> Finish this sentence: I wish I were more _____.
>
> Talk about an embarrassing moment.

An interesting guest one year was a cultural anthropologist who was doing her doctoral research on menopausal women. Personal experiences and feelings, along with both myths and medical information, were discussed openly. The deep woods of Wisconsin provided a safe place for meaningful conversation. Women need safe places to talk and they also deserve good information on a subject that can be fraught with fears and foibles.

The Spa Group

This collection of five young mothers were, like most of us, unable to afford a fancy spa and the entitlement of pampering they represent. They did, however, dream of such luxury in the midst of dirty diapers and countless other demands on their time. Being an innovative group, they pooled their money and rented a hotel suite for two weekend nights in the middle of a Minnesota winter. They hired a masseuse to come one afternoon to relax their weary muscles, shared excerpts from their journals and brought along health food in an earnest effort to get in better shape. The health food was soon replaced with take-out food from a Mexican restaurant when they settled in to watch the video, *Shirley Valentine.* Shirley is an English woman with a large heart and a fascination for Greece. When her husband throws his plate of food on the floor and her son and daughter make it abundantly clear that their mother is on earth simply to meet their every need, Shirley chooses another direction.

These women started talking late one evening, with Shirley Valentine's words, "My little life when there's so much more," ringing in their ears. They began to talk about their own dreams and what they wanted their future to look like. They became hesitant to talk about any skills or talents they had until, on impulse, one of the women suggested that they all think about and then write down what they knew their four friends' creative abilities to be. One thing led to another, and personal confidence began to grow, allowing them to express some of their innermost visions. One of the women opened a florist shop two years later—a direct result of the encouragement of her friends. Another went back to college to pursue her degree in counseling, a dream she had let fall by the wayside years earlier.

The Flower Ladies

These women are another group of five who, already good friends, attended an all-day seminar on flower arranging at Northwestern University. Arriving at the seminar, they discovered the process for the day: two people would share a table and grouped on and around each table were buckets of fresh flowers and greens, vases and bowls, green foam, floral wire and moss. Everyone was given a challenge and vision for their project and told that each layer should stand alone for its expression of beauty. If the green foam and greenery were the first layer, it in itself would be lovely before another layer, perhaps particular flowers, was added.

The group's foundation, learned at the seminar, has never changed. Seasonally they meet and create beauty for their homes and as gifts to give family members and friends. One of the women gave her new daughter-in-law a holiday bouquet with the promise that she would receive three more arrangements throughout the year.

The women come together with their tool kits and containers, which might include wicker baskets, a small sleigh for holiday bouquets or other imaginative vases. One or two of the members take the assignment of buying flowers and greens and the cost is divided among the five.

When one of the women mentioned her fondness for Afternoon Tea, it was agreed that the combination of flower arranging and a tea party was a natural and again their creative spirits soared when they baked such things as lemon tarts and maple scones. Their husbands were included for one special holiday tea, and surrounded by glorious winter bouquets, they enjoyed an event unknown to most men.

The Spring Maiden Group

This enriching group is made up of mothers and their daughters who are approaching young womanhood. Every mother and daughter receives the following invitation when the daughter to be recognized is thirteen years old.

> *Would you please bring the following symbolic gifts:*
>
> *A fresh flower that reminds you of my daughter and the reasons you chose that particular flower.*
>
> *A dish for our potluck dinner. An old family recipe would be wonderful. Please write out the recipe on one of the enclosed index cards. These recipes will serve to start my daughters collection.*
>
> *On the second card, write down your wishes for my daughter and your recipe for happiness.*
>
> *Most of the evening will be spent hearing other women's stories. We'll talk some about our own experiences when we were thirteen and encourage our daughters to ask questions. Do you remember waking up one morning, looking into the mirror and thinking you had changed? What has it meant for you to be a daughter, sister, mother and friend?*

On one occasion, a mother brought some excerpts from *The Genteel Lady's Companion and Guide from 1889*. You can imagine the shrieks when the "qualities and attributes of feminine pulchritude and comeliness" were read aloud:

THE HEAD should be round of shape with no unsightly bumps or bulges.

THE EYEBROWS should be centered like open umbrellas over the eyes, which should be set one on either side of the nose.

THE NOSE should divide the face down the middle.

THE NECK should be as long as the head is wide.

THE SHOULDERS should be twice as wide as the head is long.

THE BOSOM should not be noticed, mentioned or discussed.

THE HANDS should be covered at all times with winter gloves, summer gloves, household gloves or bedtime mittens and the little finger of each hand should be crooked in a fetching and dainty manner.

THE TORSO should be laced, braced and corseted in a fashion that imparts grace to the carriage, elegance to the form and strength to the shoulders and back.

THE ARMS should be firm, full and well rounded at the points in order that they prove suitable for carrying, sweeping, toting, beating, scrubbing, lifting and swatting.

THE LOWER LIMBS should be clothed in such a manner that their form and shape not be distinguishable beneath the folds of the lady's many skirts.

THE ANKLE should be small and finely turned.

THE FOOT should be a delicate and delightful extension of the ankle, yet it should never be allowed to peep from beneath the lady's skirts, for the mere exposure of the foot, no matter how fine, besmirches the mantle of modesty in which a lady of genteel ways should always be clothed.

You can only imagine how incredulous the young girls were, and there was more to come. A letter to Miss Lydia during the same year of 1889:

Dear Miss Lydia,
I am up at four in the morning to milk the cow and feed the barnyard animals; then I prepare my husband's breakfast; then I clean the floors, windows, rugs, furnishings and furniture of nineteen rooms; then I sew, mend, garden, bake and cook my husbands dinner. My husband says I look thin and I appear distraught. What can I do?
Ellen

Miss Lydia's response:

Ellen, a thin face with hard lines and sunken cheeks is not an attractive face with which to greet your husband at the breakfast table. Thinness in a woman also betrays a sharp and fretful nature and nervous and bilious disorders. I heartily recommend Dr. Dextor Fedor's Vegetable Compound Pills taken thrice daily to combat irritability and nervousness and to stimulate the appetite.

One can only wonder if Miss Lydia was really a woman!

The Moon Group

This group was the inspiration of six mothers, all of whom home school their children. All had daughters who were approaching womanhood and on the verge of their first menstrual period—hence the name. I understand that there is no subject unanswered within this group and menstrual periods are a cause for celebration, as each daughter, in turn, is welcomed into the world of women. These marvelous celebrations are a mixture of spirituality and the wisdom of women, gathered from their readings and their own intuitive natures. The experiences of the mothers, both humorous and painful, are passed on to the daughters, along with antiquated myths and superstitions, building a new and stronger level of both knowledge and self-confidence, an extraordinary gift from a mother to her daughter. The fathers are, on occasion, invited to their meetings and plans are underway for an evening where fathers and daughters will prepare a meal together.

Their husbands and sons have formed a similar group. Young men will talk about their own entry into manhood, respect for young girls and women and character building. They call themselves the Sun Group.

The bedrock of self-confidence, knowledge and personal responsibility resonates in both groups, all encompassed by loving parents and friends.

Coming of Age

When I heard about this gathering it involved an eighteen-year-old boy and his extended family of men—a father, grandfathers, uncles and cousins. The father brought everyone together for what he called A Walk to Manhood. They meet for an afternoon, dinner and an evening. The only instruction the father gave was that each man take his son aside and teach him some things they felt he ought to know. Intriguing.

Since a good idea should be shared, what about time like this for a daughter who is off to college, approaching her first job or getting married?

The Babes

This group came to be when all the young women were pregnant and met at a birthing class. The leader of the class was a midwife, also expecting her first child. I heard about their joyful dancing with colorful scarves a few weeks before their labors and wondered how this festive behavior may have affected their yet unborn children.

The same midwife delivered all the babies in a hospital and they made a commitment to meet monthly to ask questions and talk about their experiences. They found that two of the women were experiencing post partum depression (baby blues), and some needed assistance and encouragement for their desire to breast feed, among countless other issues familiar to most new mothers. These women were never left adrift without loving support and good information during a time that can leave women alone, confused and frightened.

They planned mother/child trips together, short excursions, like picnics in the park that relieve the homebound feelings so familiar to many young mothers.

The Three Sisters

These women, in their thirties and forties, all lived in the same community. As luck would have it, there was a dress shop nearby that catered to brides and, in addition, sold prom and party dresses. When the shop held their final, FINAL clearance sale, the sisters went shopping! This was a yearly event for them and, since only the most ghastly bridesmaid and floozy prom dresses were on sale, the sisters had a picnic trying on the creations and always bought one or two each. Why? Why not? The dresses were so cheap and who knows how they might come in handy in the future?

Some years passed and each sister had seven or eight unworn dresses hanging in their closets. Then an opportunity presented itself. *Fiddler on the Roof* was coming to a neighboring community and the sisters convinced their parents, husbands and children to go together on opening night. And to go in style.

The men in their family were enthusiastic rather than reluctant victims and their father, from whence came their genes, rented a tux, cane and top hat. The three generations of women spread all their dresses out on beds, and, not unlike the southern belles in **Gone with the Wind,** tried on dresses amid gales of laughter until they found the one that especially suited them.

The whole tribe, seventeen strong, went to opening night and then retired to their parents' home where they danced and ate food that had been prepared before the big event. Imagine the memories their family had built, all because of a clearance sale and three lively sisters.

I once read, "There are only two kinds of people in the world. Those that are alive and those that are fearful." It is my belief that women's groups, whatever their makeup (and two women together certainly count), are among the most alive people in the universe.

When I heard about the Moon group, the Spring Maiden parties, the Sun Group and the Coming of Age celebrations, I thought again about the value of mentors, role models and nutritious parents, those men and women who are within reach, both physically and emotionally for young girls and boys. Children need loving and self-confident adults who are not afraid to create opportunities for both intimacy and truth telling, thereby creating a safe place to question and discover.

The opportunities that may make a girl's teenage years more comfortable are ours to construct. Perhaps somewhere there are Barbie-doll like girls who float through their teenage years without a qualm about their physical appearances, approval or acceptance by their peers, but I doubt it.

However hidden, we all suffer a great deal of self-doubt and wild mood swings. We've all had times when we could rival Sarah Bernhardt's dramatic acting and, if weren't outwardly rebelling, we were often looking for a cause to complain about. We knew as teens that nobody understood us except, again, our close girlfriends.

I was one of those girls who, when sides were being picked for some sports event, was one of the last chosen. Do you know how difficult it is to stand there with a lump in your throat and a dumb smile on your face?

Mary Grewe, of The Roses and I shared a similar dark past. Together we amassed a collection of embarrassing and farcical sporting stories. Golf and tennis were simply not possible for us. We thought it had something to do with our reaction time. Slow. To give some hope and encouragement to younger women who can identify with us, we found a sport on one of the Roses' trips we loved—whitewater rafting.

As women we need to tell our truths to our daughters and sons, and encourage their fathers to do the same. Family or group support may offer further enriching opportunities.

Start Your Engines

The following exercises can be wonderful fun for small groups of women who believe they know each other quite well.

Getting to Know You Better

Write down four things about yourself that even your close friends are not aware of. These things can be about your birth family, ancestors, past experiences and even future hopes or aspirations. Anything goes.

Three will be true and one of your statements false.

Let your friends try to figure out which one is false.

They probably will want more information about your true statements too. I remember a woman in a workshop stating that her grandmother was a can-can dancer in France. That was one of her true statements. Have fun!

Here's what Cynthia, 64 wrote:

1) *I studied and loved fashion illustration in college.*
2) *After being raised by a minister and attending a girls' boarding school, run by nuns, I seriously considered becoming a nun myself.*
3) *I played the violin for four years.*
4) *I've worked since I was thirteen. Work that included cleaning toilets, washing dishes, making beds and waiting on tables for a conference center.*

(Number 2 is false)

Collaboration

You'll need at least four women for this one and knowledge of the interests and abilities of each will be important.

If you were going to decorate a room, which of your friends would you call on for help and why?

If you were writing a book for women, who would you call on for help and why?

If you were making a movie?

If you were opening a bookstore?

If you needed someone to talk to your troubled teenager?

If you needed to dress for a special event?

If you needed to create an outfit for a Halloween party?

If you were undecided about your hair and make-up?

Are You More Like

Characteristics and behaviors will come to mind as you begin to talk. If you do this exercise with another woman or a group of women, let the others respond to what they believe to be true about the woman who has chosen to talk *before* she gives characteristics that she believes to be true about herself. You might be amazed and delighted by the feedback, as others are bound to see you in a somewhat different light.

Are you more like:

- A wildflower or a hothouse orchid?
- A back road or a super highway?
- A jeep or a convertible?
- A caterpillar or a butterfly?
- A comedy or a tragedy?
- A lake or a river?
- Roots or branches?
- Shirley Valentine or Saint Valentine?
- Scarlett or Melanie?
- A merry-go-round or a roller coaster?
- A front porch or a backyard patio?
- A bulldozer or a dump truck?
- A country tavern or a New York restaurant?

Personally, I'd like to be thought of as a front porch rather than a backyard patio. I still have fond memories of people sitting on front porches and visiting with neighbors as they walked by, swinging on an old-fashioned glider with a parent or playing there on a rainy day. A backyard patio speaks to me of hiding from only the invited people and eating outside surrounded by little biting bugs.

Looking at the same two things from a different angle, I might say that I'd like to be thought of as a backyard patio because I enjoy spending time with close friends and, for me, a front porch is like being a sitting duck for anybody that happens to walk by.

Lucy, 15 wrote her response to, "Are you more like a lake or a river?"

"At this stage of my life, I feel more like a river than a lake. A river is going somewhere—though WHERE is not always apparent. Like me, a river changes from day to day. Sometimes it is calm and contented, in no hurry to reach its destination, relishing every moment of its journey. At other times, it rushes impatiently toward its goal, tenaciously shoving aside anything in its way. A lake is more settled, because it has no desire to do anything that would disrupt the tranquility it has found. Only its surface can be ruffled, leaving the deepest parts still and quiet. I hope and try to maintain a balance between river characteristics and lake characteristics because its important to me to have the determination of a river, as well as the serenity of a lake."

Kay, 64, wrote her response to, "Are you more like a merry-go-round or a roller coaster?"

"My life is like a roller coaster—up and down, down and up. One day I feel on top of the world and the next day I'm at the bottom. When I'm in the middle, I'm giddy and excited about what lies ahead. It's an ever-changing life and I find that wonderful! There is rarely a dull moment, which means I don't often become bored. If I were asked what I have the most of, it would be up days. I am blessed with friends who come from the same ilk."

Now we're going to take a little detour and listen to the poetic musings of some other women. Beats a car radio!

Chapter Five
Some Traveling Companions

"One woman understands another."
Irish Proverb

These writings are by women friends and daughters who, seeking to better appreciate their own awakenings, joys and challenges, may mirror some of your thoughts and experiences. Poetry often is a gift of the spirit from one woman to another giving solace and sanction when we sometimes feel alone, unappreciated or misunderstood.

Friends

We are individual,
We are each other,
Years have brought us
Together in threads
Of various talents,
Strengths, personalities
Sizes and shapes—
Even ordinary things
Into a fabric of
Synergized beauty.
Sometimes fine, delicate,
Or course linsey-woolsey
Textures of each other.
The warp and woof.
The collective joy
In best of friends.

Yvonne Brunstad

A Voice Regained

She had a remarkable voice
clear and true and vibrant.
A voice mellowed by time and tempo.
So unique was her voice, that several members of the choir
approached her. "Please join our choir. We need your voice
to round out our sound."
And she did, with great enthusiasm and high anticipation.
When practices began, her voice rang out!
Soon, the senior members of the choir began to murmur.
"Tone down."
"Not that loud."
"No, not that sonata."

And the choir director joined in,
"No solos, yet. You must first learn to blend with the choir."

And her songs were not sung
and her vibrancy was gone
and her tone became flat
and her tempo was slowed
and the music within her was silenced
and she sang without soul.

Until the day she decided to set her own rhythm
and explore her full range and to sing her own music again.
And she regained her voice!

And the choir wondered how she could leave the security
of their loft.
Years later, when her voice had fully ripened
and was recognized throughout the land, she realized:

Not everyone is meant to sing in the choir.

Christy L. Schwan

The Wheel

The Hub
who finds comfort in routine
in being unhurried
in being anchored
in being encompassed
in balancing and supporting
in observing and waiting

The Spokes
who are capable
of going in many directions simultaneously
in being part of many lives
in accomplishing many tasks
in giving much
in loving much
in needing much
whose many facets return and focus
at a common source

All enveloped by the Rim
the intangibles
the collection of circumstances
the depth
the intimacy
the promise
the possibilities
the love
All woven into a gossamer cocoon
with the strength of steel.

Diane Garber

My Christmas Letter

'Twas the month before Christmas
And all through the house,
I was naughty, wrong, incompetent,
An all around louse!

Now this was not new,
I had heard this before,
On a regular basis,
For 13 years or more.

I've worked to improve,
And to fix this disaster,
But there's not one thing,
I've yet to master.

My failures are far too numerous to list,
But I'll give you a few,
Just so you get the gist . . .

My house is not orderly,
The pencil drawer's a mess!
And where are the scissors?
It's anyone's guess.

I don't keep a running inventory of stuff.
Do I need dish soap? Tomato sauce? Puffs?

There are many more examples,
Like "what supplies I have stored."
But I'll move along now,
Lest you get bored.

Lessons, lectures, corrections,
He tried to teach me a lot.
The more I did,
The worse I got.

My areas of weakness,
Are widespread and diverse.
Being married to me,
Why what could be worse!

He does not deserve someone of my ilk.
I let the kids sleep in!
I give them cereal and milk!

I snuggle them at bedtime,
Until way too late,
And I help them too much,
Why he's NINE and she's EIGHT!

I can't seem to get it,
Everything's a big deal,
If I'd just do things his way,
No matter how I feel.

So my message to you,
Through this Christmas letter,
Is I'm making a plan,
To make future years better.

Merry Christmas! Glad tidings! Be of good cheer!

I'm leaving this guy the first of the year.

Barbara Westrate

A Young Woman Becoming Aware of Her Inner Strength

Am I a witch
with chants and spells
magic potions,
thunder quells?

For when I think,
Or read or write
the mystery gathers
dulling light.

As miraculous as
wingless flight
or life from death
or eyeless sight,

The new connections
in my mind
As powers great
the lies unwind.

And so I wonder
why we fret
at lacking powers
fairies get.

Margaret Fleming Sirianni

Burnt Offerings

I wouldn't let him stop. Steeped in anger, I forced him to drive on in silence. His hunger eventually overtook him and he pulled into the truck stop, bought food which I refused to eat. He wolfed it down between his tears as I sat stone-like.

How could he not understand my need to spontaneously celebrate our anniversary? I'd laid out a general path for our trek home, subtly planning to stop by places we'd always wanted to visit, but never had the time to explore. Surely we'd find a wonderful place to have dinner and spend the night. Surely he'd see the benefit of giving up his mission.

His mission. His mission was paramount. Return the van by 4 PM. Return the van by 4 PM. The litany was so fitting.

I wouldn't let him stop until after midnight. Our anniversary officially ended. Destroyed. Beyond recovery. Memorable in its anger.

Why couldn't I stop myself? Why did I need to punish him so? He wanted desperately to please me. And that was the problem. I wanted him to want what I wanted. I didn't want him to appease me. Give in to me. I wanted him to surprise me, make the decision, lay out the plan, take charge.

I'm tired of being the cruise director, the activity chairman, the party planner. I'd wanted him to think up our next excursion and the perfect place to start was our anniversary.

As usual, we made up. Confessing our love but neither of us forgiving. He's really a sensitive and sentimental person. I hurt him deeply by my refusal to accept his burnt offerings, his willingness to turn back to the place where I had envisioned staying. But the dream was mine, not his. His understanding came too late and our misunderstanding adds another stone to our marriage altar.

Christy L. Schwan

Real Self

Who is who
They appear to be?
I see faces quite serene,
Like mine is, (I think)—
Yet is it possible
They suffer like me?

I am so vulnerable
With every encounter:
I come to these meetings
Drained, yet anticipating.

She appears to
Have it all together,
But don't I?
And will I ever?

I want to speak
About my inner self,
The woman I like.
I have something to offer
And want to share.

My thoughts and dreams,
The good things about life,
What I like to do,
And the goals I have.

But I'm wondering . . .
It's possible that she
Could be living and feeling
My same thoughts?

So I must ask her,
"How are you doing?"
With sincerity, so she
Knows I care.
Then she might open
Her heart, then
I can too.

Yvonne Brunstad

Limmericks

Grandmother Bold

There once was a grandmother bold
Who loved to go out in the cold.
Cold air made her blurt,
"This keeps me alert!
I'm glad I'm so bold when I'm old!"

Retired Required

A woman whose husband retired
Was stunned at the time he required
With him under foot—
Her schedule Ka Putt
She wished he was back to rehired!

Yvonne Brunstad

A Young Woman's Poem to Her Father on Her Birthday

Though it may not always be clear
The things that are most
Important in life
I've learned from you.

And sometimes the presence of fear
Your reaction to the things that I do

A crunch of a pickle
An overspent nickel
A stolen condiment

Makes it hard to communicate on a level that's true.

So when I say it's black
And you say it's blue
While I'm finding my way
Sometimes I forget . . . you are, too.

Katherine Fleming

A Wife to Her Husband

In Pecos the Indians
Built on a rock.
So have
You.

My rock has given me
A foundation,
Support,
Security,
Protection.

From it I am able,
To view the world,
Expand my horizons,
Nourish others,
Create life.

I could not do this
Without my rock.
I am grateful.
I love you.

Lois Postelwaite

Alone

She's been wheeled away
For surgery
And I'm afraid for her.
But I only wait—
What's on her mind
As she faces her fate?
Old friends we are,
With long, good memories.
So easy for us to be together
Yet now we're alone.

Together in thought
But alone.

Yvonne Brunstad

Chapter Six
Help, Don't Honk

I write letters to my grandchildren because I know the importance of expressing love and encouragement in a letter. These are letters that might be read throughout a persons life, or whenever there is a need for emotional support and a connection to someone who loved you unconditionally.

My mother and father never spent a night away from each other throughout their married life. Working together in a small hardware store, they spent a good deal of time with each other. Consequently, there was never an opportunity to write letters between them. Yet, my dad would, every once in awhile, leave love notes for my mother in the mailbox. I have no idea as to what caused him to do this other than the fact that it was a sweet thing to do and he was a sweet man.

My mother always said that she too would write him a letter someday. Fate has a way of directing lives, because she did write him a letter, six months before she died very suddenly and with no prior warning. In her letter she wrote about her love for him and their family, the people their children married, their grandchildren and the years they had spent together. He gathered toys for children that he knew would have little or nothing under their tree. She wrote about watching him leave the house a few nights before Christmas, dressed as Santa and with a sack slung over his back.

My sister, brother and I knew of the letter but had never read it. It was a personal letter for his eyes only.

My dad died thirteen months after my mother's death. In the weeks that followed his death we had the heart-rending task of clearing their home and choosing what we wanted to take from it. There were few things of monetary value but others that brought back lovely memories of a warm and close family. Any of you who have had this experience will understand the avalanche of emotions and sadness that overwhelms you. We were all, however, focused on one thing: finding my mother's letter to Dad.

We discovered it and it is in my possession today. I read it now and again and it is a constant reminder of their love and devotion for each other. It is a legacy to cherish.

The importance of finding my mother's letter is why I have written the following letters. I want to leave my words for nine remarkable human beings to read whenever it suits them.

At the time of this writing Lucy is fifteen and Grace and Rose are nine years old. Mike is seventeen, Kal and Ned are fifteen, Sam and Will are thirteen and Milo is six years old.

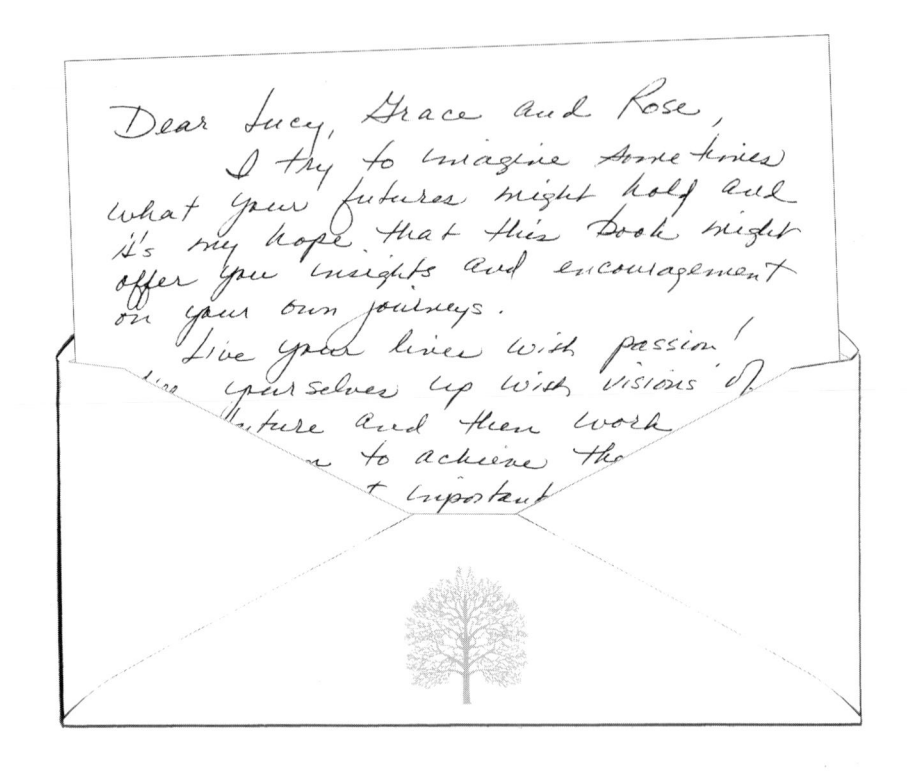

> Dear Lucy, Grace and Rose,
> I try to imagine sometimes what your futures might hold and it's my hope that this book might offer you insights and encouragement on your own journeys.
> Live your lives with passion! ... yourselves up with visions of ... future and then work ... to achieve the ... important

Dear Lucy, Grace and Rose,

I try to imagine sometimes what your futures might hold and it's my hope that this book might offer you insights and encouragement on your own journeys.

Live your lives with passion! Fill yourselves up with visions of your future and then work as hard as you can to achieve the ones that are most important to you. Dream and imagine how you would like to see your life unfold.

You'll all have many choices to make throughout your lives. I urge you to think about them with your head as well as with your heart and heed the wisdom your parents will offer. Consider the consequences of your decisions.

When you have disappointments, give yourself a pat on the back for doing your best and then buck up and keep trying if what you're after is important to you. You will be amazed with the power of perseverance.

Be virtuous and respect your bodies.

Be as loving as you can because every single person you know and even people you have just met—need your kindness and compassion. Strive for empathy because we live in a world where too many people enjoy judging others. Fill others up with your thoughtfulness and attempt to see how things look from another persons point of view.

Continue to be avid readers, and include books about the experiences of other women. You will then continue to grow, throughout your lives, in self-awareness and personal responsibility.

Our family circle is strong. We all hold hands with the people who have gone before and those who are yet to be born. What you do or don't do will have its impact on others, most especially your parents and your future husbands and children. May your places in our circle reflect vital, trustworthy, radiant and caring women. Look for humor in almost all situations because that will sustain you and always be willing to laugh at yourself.

Regardless of your career successes always remember that your relationships with the people you love will be the most important thing in your lives.

I treasure all of you. Know that I will love you forever,

Grandma Joan

Dear Mike, Ned, Kal, Sam, Will and Milo,

It's very important for me to write you some of my thoughts. Most probably you will all be husbands and fathers in the future and I'd like to get my two cents worth in!

I'll start by telling you a big secret. Do you know what many girls and women find most attractive in a man? In my seventy years of life experience, the answer is a man who can express his feelings. When a man talks about his challenges, fears and even what moves him to tears, women see strength.

I've asked a good number of women what they look for in a loving relationship with a man and the answers I hear most often are:

A man who enjoys being around and playing with children.
A man who is kind to animals.
A man who treats girls and women with respect.
A man who has a great sense of humor.

These qualities allow women to know that a man is both self-confident and caring. A self-confident man is a man of integrity and integrity is the value you place on yourself.

Do you know that every time you're with another person you have a choice to either build them up or break them down? There isn't a woman in the world who can't tell you a story of how a young man hurt her feelings or destroyed her self-esteem when she was a young girl or in high school.

Isn't that amazing?

Look for times when you can help other people feel better about themselves.

Discover a career that will give you great satisfaction and joy. It is well worth your time and effort to think deeply about this because it will greatly affect the quality of your lives. When you are pleased with your choice of career, you will live with abundance and become a superb role model for your children and those who know you.

Always rely on the people within our family. We circle the wagons when someone has a problem or crisis and we help each other. I think that your experiences at Boot Camp with your grandfather, fathers and uncles will continue long into the future. The make-up of the groups may change—including your own sons—but it's my hope that the spirit of men and boys having adventures together never changes.

When I am with you now, either individually or as a group, my heart swells with pride. In a nutshell, keep on being the young men of character and personal responsibility I love so dearly.

Grandma Jean

Acknowledgements

There are people in my life that have been with me as I have written this book; people whose spirits I want to recognize.

My editor and friend, Barbara Winter whose keen eye for detail and ability to help me sort out my thoughts made this book a reality. We are often synergy in action!

Her newsletter, *Winning Ways* and her book, *Making a Living Without a Job* reflect her joyful lifestyle. You can find out more at *www.barbarawinter.com*.

Jane Evershed, an artist for positive social change. A detail from her signature painting, "Leap of Faith Woman," appears on the back cover. She can be reached at *www.evershed.com*.

The Big Four includes Dorothy Wheeler, Dixie Fixmer and Pat Branigan.

The Roses includes Sue Kristo, Jacque Falk and the late Mary Grewe.

The Lavender Hill Mob includes Cynthia Larson, Yvonne Brunstad and Barbara Ludins. Yvonne's book, *It Could be Verse*, can be ordered from her: Yvonne Brunstad, 679 Cedarwood Court, Chippewa Falls, Wisconsin, 54729

Nancy Kloss, my college friend.

Shirley Decker, my sister-in-law, whose inspiration for the title of this book really grabbed me. She has a fairy walk in the woods in front of her home that, when the scrolled wrought iron gate is open, her grandchildren can enter and begin their walk along a winding path. There are surprises in alcoves and after a sudden turn in the path you just might spot a woodland creature high in a pine tree. I enjoyed a whispered walk with her granddaughter, Sarah, whose imagination knew there was magic on the path and wanted me to watch for the fairies with her.

Paula Kadanec and Mary Grewe were lifelong friends and for years gave each other silly, goofy gifts on each other's birthdays, sometimes trying to out gross the other. They were a part of a larger birthday group and Paula believed a bit of levity was needed and that Mary would be the perfect foil. Together they created a zany tradition. Paula's first gift to Mary was a lovely dresser-set hairbrush—adorned with the first owner's hair! Their mutual gifts were from their own closets, flea markets or were double gifted, providing the original gift giver was not identified. In another effort to keep Mary's memory alive, Paula and I, friends for over thirty-five years, now carry on this tradition and I've found firsthand how ingenious Paula is. Knowing how I enjoy the sun, she gifted me with a huge straw hat that was the product of a memorable sailboat trip. Perched on the top are multi-colored zinnias, giving it panache!

Mary Taylor of the Flower Ladies, a woman who always encourages the creative efforts of her friends, and I am grateful to be one of her friends. I spent a day with these imaginative women in our local florist shop, Avalon, and was amazed, not only at the way they put their arrangements together, but at the delight they found in each other's decorations. It was a joyful day!

My sister-in-law Margaret Schneider and her daughters, Elena, Julie and Mia. Together with our family of women and men, who go along with our madcap ideas, we continue to enjoy memorable family times together. One of the best has been our appetizer contests. Instead of a joint meal, everyone makes an appetizer that will be judged by the group for presentation as well as taste. When inspired grandchildren join in, this is indeed an evening to be remembered. On one occasion this feast was accompanied by dressing up. Among the most unique was a sleazy woman of the night wearing a black silk slip with a dog collar around her neck and a flamboyant woman with sparkly eye make-up. My husband Dick came up with a rather unusual appetizer during one such event and named it Celtic Famine Nuggets. According to him it was introduced during the potato famine in Ireland, the country of some of his forefathers. He concocted this masterpiece out of leftovers in the refrigerator and rated high in presentation although not in taste.

My friend Johanna Warloski. Few feelings are left unspoken between us.

My sister Ruth Stevens who is known within our family circle for her generosity—most notably the time she spends with her nieces and nephews, encouraging their knowledge and love of animals. Her therapy dogs have inspired others within the family to train and certify their own dogs.

My daughters:

Anne Charnley, an RN at the National Center for Post Traumatic Stress Disorders,

Kate Fleming, a high school English teacher with a teenage son,

Meg Sirianni, a home schooling mother of four, and

Molly Button, mother of four and a children's librarian.

My husband, Dick. He is a man of integrity and character—and he unquestionably is a character! He can always be counted on to be in our corner—as a husband, father and grandfather.

From My Bookcase

Books that have inspired and those that I read a second or third time . . .

My all time favorite is *East of Eden* by John Steinbeck.

Divine Secrets of the Ya Ya Sisterhood by Rebecca Wells

Talk Before Sleep by Elizabeth Berg

My Grandfather's Blessing by Rachel Naomi Remen M.D.

Wild Mind by Natalie Goldberg

So You Want to Write by Brenda Uleland

Gift From the Sea by Anne Morrow Lindbergh

All of Anne Perry's Victorian mysteries. Her characterizations of both men and women are marvelous.

The Red Tent and *Good Harbor* by Anita Diamant

The Secret Life of Bees by Sue Monk Kidd

Angry Housewives Eating Bon Bons and *Patty Jane's House of Curl* by Lorna Landvik

The Second Shift by Arlie Hochschild

Women's Reality by Anne Wilson Schaef

Peoplemaking by Virginia Satir

I Would Love to Hear Your Story

This has been a work of non-fiction and my words along with those of the many women contained within are true. I know that every reader has their own story and I am eager to hear them.

Do you belong to a woman's group? Would you write to me and tell me about your experience?

Have you made a personal choice in your life that impacted on the direction your life has taken?

Do you have wisdom you'd be willing to pass on to others, the result of your life experiences?

Do you have a passion? Perhaps one that is still in the dream stage or one that is well underway?

Write to me:

>Joan Fleming
>8705 Rambil Road
>Eau Claire, Wisconsin 54703

>e-mail: joan@anybody.com

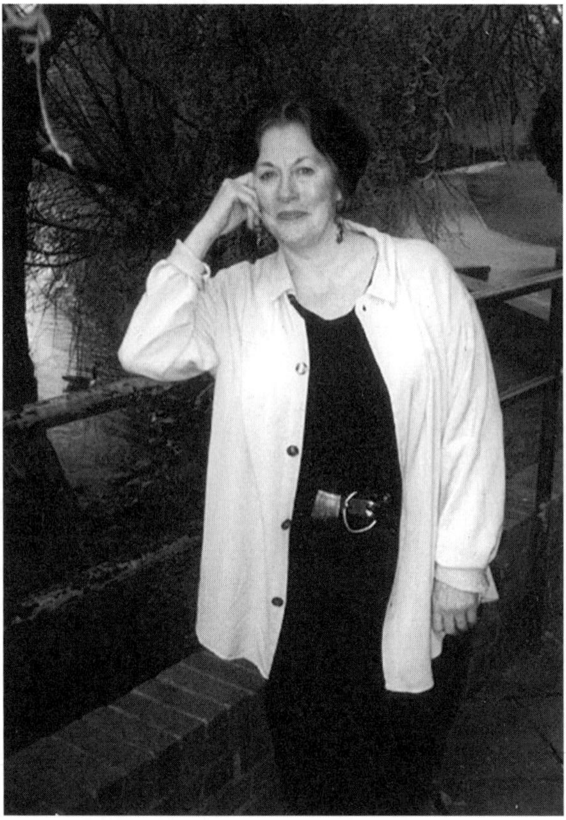

About the Author

Joan Fleming has presented talks and workshops for women for over thirty years. These workshops are all variations of her zestful women research and her own life experiences—most especially with her four daughters and women friends.

She has been married for fifty years and she and Dick enjoy nine grandchildren. Joan wrote *Papa's Legacy, The Growing of GRANDchildren*. The purpose of this book is to strengthen already loving relationships between the generations. She writes about grandparents leaving a zestful legacy, and includes character-building discussions between grandparents and grandchildren along with ideas for people who live far from their grandchildren and still long to be a force for good in their lives.

Joan would rather swim than cook. Fortunately she married a man who loves to cook, although his passion was a process that grew over the years.

Order Form

To order additional copies of **Fuel Stop**: Send check or money order for $18.95 per book (includes mailing) to the address below. How would you like *Fuel Stop* autographed?

_____

_____

To order Joan Fleming's book, **Papa's Legacy: The Growing of GRANDchildren**, send check or money order for $16.95 per book (includes mailing) to the address below. How would you like *Papa's Legacy* autographed?

_____

_____

For a set of both books, send $33.00.

These books are available at special quantity discounts to use as:
- Fund raising for women's groups
- Women's book clubs
- Sales promotions
- Gifts for employees

Contact Joan Fleming (see below) for more information

Title	Quantity		Total
Fuel Stop		× $18.95	
Papa's Legacy		× $16.95	
Set of both		× $33.00	
		Order total	

Send check or money order payable to Joan Fleming to:

Joan Fleming
8705 Rambil Road
Eau Claire, Wisconsin 54703

e-mail: joan@anybody.com